"Confident, authentic, and engaging presentations are critical for success in business and in life. *Talk on Water* can help any speaker hone and improve his or her communication skills. This book provides you with specific, actionable advice that you can apply immediately. The key concepts are clear and based on sound logic and research. I recommend this book to my students and coaching clients alike."

—MATT ABRAHAMS, author of *Speaking Up without Freaking Out,* lecturer, Stanford Graduate School of Business

"*Talk on Water* covers all the bases for becoming a confident, prepared, and engaging presenter. Stephanie's practical and original perspective, combined with her passion as a coach, makes *Talk on Water* a reader-friendly, positive experience."

—LAURIE SCHLOFF, executive communication coach, The Speech Improvement Company, Inc.

"Brilliant, inspiring, and rewarding. Scotti's perspective and expertise make for an enjoyable, thought-provoking, and transformational read. A great book for anyone seeking a competitive advantage or simply looking to elevate their personal brand."

—MICHAEL C. ROSONE, VP of service sales and marketing, Arista

"*Talk on Water* is a must-read for anyone who wants to move from being an adequate presenter to an exceptional one. Stephanie's advice is practical and actionable with a focus on authenticity— which is, at the core, the secret sauce to any impactful presentation."

—KARIN REED, author of *On-Camera Coach*; CEO, Speaker Dynamics

"*Talk on Water* is for business leaders looking to get more traction from their presentations. Stephanie's amazing insight and unique approach in assigning purpose to the presenter is nothing short of game-changing. If your team wants to present to win, put her concept in your playbook and keep it there."

—BILL HARPER, CEO and chief creative officer, wmHarper

Talk
on
Water

Stephanie Dietto
May 2020

Talk
on
Water

ATTAINING THE MINDSET
FOR POWERHOUSE
PRESENTATIONS

STEPHANIE SCOTTI

WITH KARIN S. WIBERG

CLEARSIGHT
BOOKS

Published by Clear Sight Books, Raleigh, North Carolina
First edition: September 2018

ISBN: 978-1-945209-02-4
ISBN: 978-1-945209-03-1 (ebook)
Library of Congress Control Number: 2018952167

To learn more, visit professionallyspeaking.net.
For information about special discounts on bulk purchases, contact info@professionallyspeaking.net.
C.O.D.E., Talk on Water, and Presentation Profiling are trademarks of Professionally Speaking Consulting, LLC.

Book & Cover Design: Patricia Saxton
Printed in the United States of America

To my father, who taught me what it means to talk on water.

Stephen G. Scotti

1923 – 2017

Table of Contents

"I felt like anything was possible. I felt like I could walk on water—or rather, talk on water."

I grew up an Army brat, moving for the first time when I was just three days old—from Frankfurt, Germany, to Asmara, Eritrea—and then every two or three years thereafter. Each time I began to solidify a circle of friends, the geographic rug would be pulled out from under my feet. Between moving frequently and living on an enlisted man's (eventually an officer's) modest salary, I never got music or dance lessons—but I was so intent on making new friends, I didn't care. In fact, I was surprised to realize it was possible to take those types of lessons. Not having participated in dance recitals or choir concerts, I'd never been center stage—at least not until Mrs. Griffith's tenth-grade public speaking class.

Over the first few weeks of class, she taught us to stand tall, make direct eye contact, use vocal variety, and gesture broadly. She guided us in organizing our thoughts and stating a clear purpose. We practiced our new skills on several small speeches, and then got our big assignment: a three-minute speech about patriotism for the Voice of Democracy contest sponsored by the Veterans of Foreign Wars (VFW). I sat through classmate after classmate's presentation, watching and cheering them on, and offering feedback during the post-presentation critique. Finally, it was my turn.

I stood up and began my speech, attempting to use all the skills Mrs. Griffith had taught us. About sixty seconds into my talk, I sensed a shift. I noticed my classmates leaning forward, paying attention. After years of intently listening to others in an attempt to make friends, I realized people now were listening to *me*. Encouraged, I went on, using every resource I had to communicate my message. With each word, each phrase, I felt my audience drawing closer. I concluded and, rather than retreat to my desk, I again did what Mrs. Griffith taught us: I paused, looked at my peers, and smiled (silently counting "1-2-3"). Then came the applause—the first spontaneous round of applause anyone in our class had been given. Stunned, I felt an incredible connection with everyone in the room. In that moment of connection, I felt *worthy*.

Receiving that peer recognition, I felt like anything was possible. I felt like I could walk on water—or rather *talk* on water—and it became my life's mission to share that possibility with others. I believe we all have a desire for that kind of profound connection. And I believe we all have the ability to make it happen.

In high school, I began coaching classmates for speech competitions. My first "clients," Jean and Joan (twins and two of my best friends), nailed it every time. I continued coaching my peers in college-level forensic competitions, and I realized I got as much satisfaction from preparing others to speak as I did from speaking myself—maybe more.

After college, I worked for the largest speakers' bureau in the federal government preparing mid-level managers through White House staff to speak on energy policy. At age twenty-four, I coached the President's Cabinet; I'm still amazed they listened to me. Intimidated at first, I quickly learned these weren't haughty elites. They were human. They were natural, open, and committed to communicating the new policy to the country. Having this experience at such a formative point in my career gave me the confidence to work with people at the highest levels in both public and private sectors.

I went on to complete a master's degree in organizational communication and business, and I worked in the corporate world in a variety of roles. Much of that work involved helping executives prepare for high-stakes events—from pitching business to testifying on Capitol Hill—if not as part of my formal role, then informally.

Reflecting on my career experience, I realize my success goes back to that moment of truth, to that connection I felt in Mrs. Griffith's classroom. That day in tenth grade I learned a truth that has guided my practice: to be truly successful when you speak, you must connect—with yourself, your message, and your listeners.

The Link between Connection and Opportunity

Unfortunately, many of us have our heads filled with so much "stuff" about public speaking that we forget we're talking to real people. Some of us become so fearful, we're almost paralyzed. Our shaking legs and racing hearts get in the way of simply talking. Our doubts cause us to appear preoccupied as we go to our mental file cabinet to check and recheck our facts. Or, at the other extreme, we charge through our talk focused on getting our information into the world, regardless of the audience response.

When we don't connect with ourselves, our message, and our audience, we miss opportunities. We miss the chance to be authentic and in the moment. We miss the chance to communicate with purpose and to impact the world in a meaningful way. We miss the chance to feel that anything is possible.

During my years in the corporate world, I saw these missed opportunities translate into:

- Lost business when the sales team overwhelmed the potential client with details of features and benefits and locations and services and capabilities and…on and on and on.

- Wasted money on town hall meetings that didn't make a difference for employee understanding or engagement.

- Failed change management initiatives because employees didn't understand their role in making change happen.

- Lackluster product launches because the market research team talked about numbers rather than meaning and impact.

- Poor advocacy when the real-life implications of policy proposals weren't understood by legislators or regulators.

- Shallow bench strength because the new VP hadn't found her voice and the middle manager didn't know how to move beyond his subject-matter expertise.

- Negative market impact when analysts didn't understand (or didn't trust) the voices behind the numbers.

If you could find a way to improve business presentations, what might be possible? Increased sales? Stronger financial results? Deeper bench strength? New career opportunities? Increased confidence? Peace of mind?

What if your audience responded with "Hey, you're talking my language," "Wow, that's exactly what we needed to know," or "Got it—let's make it happen"?

What if you could talk on water?

Who This Book Is For

This book is for business leaders who give presentations when results matter. It's for business leaders who want to reach their audience with purpose-driven talks that engage and resonate. It's for business leaders who want to give powerhouse presentations.

At the start of my career, classes in public speaking, leadership, and other so-called soft skills were often considered something to tolerate, a nuisance that satisfied company policy or earned those much-needed continuing education credits. However, I quickly observed that when business leaders had a vested interest in the outcome—when they had a goal to accomplish, when they needed to *achieve results*—their interest in learning shifted. This is why I use an endgame strategy.

When I work with business leaders, together we focus on a high-stakes presentation with a specific goal they need to accomplish—acquiring the next big piece of business, launching a new product with impact, or leveraging credibility at an industry conference. The presentation skills are simply the tools to success.

What You'll Learn

This is a goal-oriented, strategic book designed to help you elevate the impact of your message and deliver it with clarity and confidence. You'll learn the strategies my clients value as they prepare for high-stakes presentations—strategies that equip them to turn "adequate" into "exceptional" in order to accomplish their objectives.

- *The Talk on Water Mindset* – Part 1 starts with a discussion of the Talk on Water™ mindset and three forms of connection. You'll learn how to succeed at being you, empathize with your audience to optimize your message, and focus on connection, not perfection.

- *Presentation Profiling* – In Part 2, you'll learn to use Presentation Profiling™ to determine which speaker profile—Expert, Interpreter, or Catalyst—will shape your success in any given presentation.

- *The Presentation C.O.D.E.* – Part 3 offers the C.O.D.E.® process to help you craft content and deliver it effectively. Even in this practical, application-focused section, we'll emphasize mindset and strategy in relation to the tools.

- *Preparing for Prime Time* – In Part 4, you'll learn secrets for preparation and rehearsal leading up to the big event and tips for managing fear and nerves.

Ultimately your presentations become part of your personal brand. By owning your presentations and by connecting with yourself, your message, and your audience, you'll be prepared to give powerhouse presentations—giving your business an unfair competitive advantage.

Are you ready to talk on water?

PART ONE
The Talk on Water Mindset

CHAPTER 1

The Talk on Water Mindset

Present your best self.

Two weeks into her new job as a VP at an iconic lifestyle brand, Carla learned she had to give a presentation at a company-wide meeting, sharing her objectives and strategic initiatives for the coming year. She had four weeks' notice to prepare. While it was only a six-minute talk, it was her debut; she needed to have a strong presence. She needed to get it right. Nearly in a panic, she confided in the president of the company how much she struggled with public speaking. When she asked for assistance preparing, he said, "Don't worry; we'll call Stephanie."

As Carla and I began working together, she shared that she'd carried a fear of public speaking throughout her school years and career. She described how her prior company had been cliquish; rather than getting coaching and support, she was criticized—which of course made her even more nervous. Despite that experience, Carla came across as credible and likeable, though a bit more reserved than most in this fashion-forward company. I wanted her to be true to herself, yet something was holding her back and I couldn't quite put my finger on it.

As Carla rehearsed, I encouraged her to experiment with bigger, bolder movements and more vocal inflection. After all, being on a stage in front of 500 employees requires a bigger presence than a conference room. She looked uncomfortable, almost stiff, as though monitoring every movement. She seemed to be forcing herself to stay "small."

When I asked, "What are you thinking about?" her eyes filled with tears. She shared that at her last company, whenever she was about to go on stage, the president would whisper in her ear, "You know you're going to fail." This went on for years.

My goal became clear: work with Carla to regain a "worthy" mindset. She needed to know that she was not going to fail—that in fact, she was going to talk on water.

Most of us have never experienced the type of distress Carla's boss caused her, and yet many of us torture ourselves with unrealistic expectations about public speaking. This chapter offers a perspective that may help reframe your thinking and lessen the mental pressure you feel prior to critical presentations.

Foundational Beliefs

When I was growing up, my dad taught me a fundamental lesson. "Stephanie," he said, "you are unique because of who you are. If you compare yourself to anyone else, you're always going to feel *less,* because there will always be someone better than you. Or you'll get too high on your horse thinking you're better than everyone else and never reach your true potential. Just be yourself."

Thanks, Dad. I'm grateful you instilled that belief in me at such a young age. As a result, I believe every person who steps up to speak is unique. Especially in a business environment, embracing your gifts and expressing your individuality is what allows you to talk on water. Embrace who you are, what you're there to do, and your commitment to doing it. If you want to improve your skills, do it for yourself, not to compare yourself with others. Just be the best you possible.

When you have confidence in who you are and what you bring to the table, you are invincible. This is the Talk on Water mindset.

Attaining a Talk on Water mindset is the differentiator that allows you to develop powerhouse presentations. Several realizations can make an enormous difference in helping you make the shift to this mindset. Keep them at the forefront as you read— they truly are foundational.

YOUR AUDIENCE IS YOUR BIGGEST FAN

Bullies aside, 99% of the time, your audience is your biggest fan. Consider the singer who hits a sour note or the comedian whose joke doesn't land. As an audience member, you want them to get better. Mentally you cheer them on (even if with a slight cringe): *Come on; you can do it!* Or, *Get on with your next joke; we'll get that one.*

Business is no different. Whether listening from choice or obligation, your audience members want to feel they're investing their time well. They don't want to be bored. They have a purpose for being there: to learn something that helps them do their job, to understand where the company is going, or to gain inspiration about their work. In the vast majority of cases, your audience is not there to judge you. They're there to hear what you have to say.

A PRESENTATION IS AN ENLARGED CONVERSATION

If you were talking with an individual or a small group at a dinner party, what would you do to have an interesting conversation? You wouldn't think too hard about gestures or vocal variety—you'd use them naturally because you'd be engaged in what you're saying and who you're speaking with. A presentation is simply an *enlarged* conversation.

The skills you use in an intimate discussion are the sames ones needed for a presentation: eye contact, an audible voice, a vocal tone that matches your words, facial expressions and gestures that match your content. Yes, when delivering a presentation you're a little farther away from your conversation partners, you speak at a more controlled pace, and you've structured your talk. And, yes, a presentation can feel one-way as you speak, but the audience does give you nonverbal feedback and audible signals (laughter or gasps), and in Q&A you get an opportunity for real back-and-forth dialog.

I'm your audience member. I'm a real person, and I want you to be a real person too. Just talk to me like we're having a conversation.

YOUR AUDIENCE WANTS CONNECTION, NOT PERFECTION

Many business speakers feel they need to put up a facade. Sometimes they hold a genuine belief that they won't be perceived as a leader unless they maintain a certain distance. Other times they feel a need for safety. We think a wall will protect us from criticism, from feeling inadequate, from revealing our vulnerabilities. A wall allows us to maintain the fiction that perfection is achievable—and if we don't achieve perfection, well then at least the arrows won't hit us. Not being perfect is difficult for some of us; we've got that professor in our head constantly judging us.

Take that pressure off yourself. Your audience does not expect or want perfection. As a matter of fact, sometimes perfection can make your audience suspicious—*What's really going on? What's he not telling us?* If you connect with them in a meaningful way, they will forgive any number of faults and listen intently. Think about yourself and how much leeway you give speakers if they've got good content and they seem to want to be there with the audience. Most people in your audience probably have a fear of speaking; they'll have empathy for you. What's the worst that could happen? You make a mistake? They've all made mistakes!

Whenever you step up to speak, remember it's all about connection, not perfection. You do have to care and connect, but you don't have to be perfect.

THERE ARE ENOUGH WAYS IN THE WORLD FOR EVERYONE TO HAVE THEIR OWN

No one wants to hear cookie-cutter speakers. Cookie-cutter speakers are *boring.* There is not *one* right way to make a business presentation; there are *many* right ways. You do not have to present like your boss or your colleague or that TED Talker who's always held up as an example. You can be yourself with your own style.

Of course, it's helpful to know the ground rules of presentations, and we'll spend some time with them later in this book. But once you know them and can use them well, you can choose where to bend them and where to flat-out break them.

Make your own best presentation your own best way, using your own natural talent. After all, there are enough ways in the world for everyone to have their own.

Dealing with Doubt

Even on your most confident of days, doubt can creep in. It can destroy your confidence as well as your credibility. Three types of doubt can sabotage you as a presenter: self-doubt, doubting your message, and doubting your audience.

Self-doubt is perhaps the most perilous: that internal nagging voice that makes you question yourself every step of the way. You start wondering, *Am I the right person to deliver this message? Do I have what it takes to drive the action that needs to occur?* Oh, the fear of judgment and of not getting it right! You get tied up in your own shorts. (An important rule to remember: Don't get tied up in your own shorts.) Every person I've ever worked with experiences self-doubt, including C-suite executives, federal government officials, celebrities, and, yes, even me. If you don't learn to manage it, self-doubt will take you down.

A close second is **doubting your message.** We've all sat through painful presentations where it was obvious the speaker had no passion for or didn't agree with the content. The fact is, content drives delivery, so if you lack confidence in your message, you stand on shaky ground. Maybe you've had to speak about a topic you're only superficially familiar with, make an announcement you don't agree with, or fill in at the last minute to deliver someone else's presentation. If you don't believe, don't care about, or are not familiar with your message, you can't expect your audience to be enthused or even interested.

Doubting your audience, the last doubt, comes in many flavors. You can doubt the audience's interest, their ability to be open-minded about a new idea, or even their ability to understand the message. *Will they do what I'm asking?* Nothing will drain your energy and suck the life out of your speech like believing no one cares what you have to say or there's no chance of moving your audience to action. Why bother if you're doomed to fail before you begin?

The overarching solution to doubt is *connection.*

- To address self-doubt, you must **connect with yourself,** so you feel grounded and can succeed at being you.

- To address message-doubt, you must **connect with the message,** making it your own while making it meaningful to the audience.

- To address audience-doubt, you must **connect with the audience,** remembering they want connection, not perfection, in both what you say and how you express your message.

Now, it's a tricky thing, this connection. All three forms work together, and all three are needed to achieve the results you want. What you will likely find is that by connecting with yourself you also better connect with your audience. But to connect with the audience you also need to connect with the message so you can connect *them* with the message. To do *that*, you need to make the message your own as well as customize it for them. And *all* that helps you connect with your own best you.

Got it?

No? Don't worry. In the next three chapters, we'll look at each form of connection.

CHAPTER 2

Connect with Yourself

Succeed at being you.

At a nonprofit organization, I gave a workshop on presentation skills most of the morning, and then had the opportunity to work one-on-one with Barbara on the speech she was giving that evening. I'd worked with Barbara several times and was familiar with her style. Her presentation was almost there, but a few areas needed refinement so we agreed to take a lunch break and then regroup.

After lunch, Barbara started rehearsing again. I watched, puzzled. Everything that she'd been doing correctly before lunch was now completely off.

I stopped her. "What happened? Between noon and 1:30 p.m., what changed?"

"Nothing," she shrugged. "Well, I got this new pair of shoes…"

"Please change them."

She did, got back up on stage, and began again.

Problem solved.

When she finished, I asked her to share her observations.

"The new shoes were so slick I thought I would fall. I got really concerned about where I stepped and how I stood."

Sometimes little things have a significant impact. Barbara's shoes made her worry about safety; they distracted her from connecting and bringing her best self to the stage.

The Importance of Connecting with Yourself

The first reason to connect with yourself is to vanquish self-doubt. The second reason, however, is to engage your audience. How so? If you aren't connected and engaged with yourself, you end up unengaged with your content. As a result you begin to sound like an adult in a Charlie Brown cartoon—"Wah wah waaah, wah wah wah-wah-wah"— which gives your audience permission to be unengaged as well. In fact, you're *asking* them to be unengaged. *Your lack of engagement gives them an out.*

So how do you connect with yourself?

Know Yourself

Knowing yourself is the crux of the Talk on Water mindset. After all, if you're not able to connect with yourself, everything else is in jeopardy. How do you see yourself? With respect to business presentations, consider two specific areas.

First, assess what you're being asked to do and your ability to do it. Are you attuned to the need and context for the presentation? Do you understand your role? Is this presentation in your comfort zone, or is it a stretch? Do you feel like the appropriate person to give it? If you have questions or qualms about the presentation or your ability to achieve the desired endgame, identify what you need to do to address those issues.

Second, recognize things that increase your concern and anxiety so you can look for ways to mitigate them. Some external elements, such as slippery shoes, are easily remedied; others, such as the venue or lighting, may be out of your control, but if you identify them in advance you can prepare for them mentally. Internal elements, such as anxiety-related physical responses, can be anticipated and mitigated too. For example, a client who gets dry mouth has learned to avoid caffeine the day before speaking since that exacerbates it. You can be nervous and even show some nervousness; just don't let the nervousness upstage you.

Give Yourself Time to Prepare

Once you step up to speak, it's all about tending to the audience. How much preparation do you need to bring your best self to the audience? What helps you feel mentally prepared? How much time and space do you need to put your thoughts together in a way that feels cohesive and makes sense to you?

Steve Jobs famously started preparing his talks months ahead of time. Most people don't have months to prepare a single business presentation. In some cases you may have twenty-four hours or less. However, when possible, try to allow yourself a reasonable span of time to develop your talk—a few days perhaps, or a few weeks for mission-critical presentations. But even in tight situations, if you can draft your speech and then walk away for twenty-four hours, you'll be able to approach it again with fresh eyes and ears; you'll see needed adjustments and feel more confident.

Focus on the Goal, Not the Performance

Professional entertainers and motivational speakers must pay attention to their performance. After all, that's what they're getting paid for: entertaining and motivating the audience. However, as a business speaker, your endgame is not the performance. Your endgame is the goal you are trying to accomplish—securing investors, gaining support for legislative issues, adopting innovative new practices.

This distinction means you don't need a choreographed, flawless performance. You need to deliver a presentation that achieves the results you want. To put it in economic terms, the marginal benefit of achieving performance perfection is unlikely to exceed the marginal cost of achieving that perfection. In other words, no one has time for detailed choreography and perfection in the business world—it's too expensive! Plus, it just doesn't feel authentic.

Let go of your feelings about the performance itself. Articulate instead the business results you want to achieve.

Then develop a clear, concise presentation that leads toward those results. Focus there. It's the best use of your energy, and it will help you get out of your head.

Keep a Bold Face & Forge Ahead

When Samsung asked Michael Bay, the action film director, to promote its new "bendy" televisions at the 2014 Consumer Electronics Show, he unintentionally caused a media frenzy. As Bay began, he looked at the teleprompter at his feet and saw the type was "all off." Flustered, he had no idea what to do and walked off the stage. From a place of empathy and years of coaching experience, I can imagine without his script he became discombobulated, froze, and slunk off in embarrassment. But it would be easy for the audience to interpret his walking off the stage as a temper tantrum.

Compare that to my client Eddie, a nervous speaker who had prepared rigorously to give a two-day seminar. Eddie had an irrational fear of tripping—he kept seeing himself falling on the steps up to the stage. Well, you know what happens when you focus on something like that: it becomes a self-fulfilling prophecy. Eddie tripped and fell flat on his face. But he jumped up, spun around, and said to the audience, "I practiced that all night... How'd I do?" You can imagine the response.

The easy lesson: Have a Plan B for easily anticipated setbacks. Eddie had prepared thoroughly for his irrational fear. Bay had not prepared for arguably the most common of presenter problems—a technology glitch!

The somewhat harder lesson: Keep a bold face and forge ahead. No matter what happens, you can handle it. As a business leader, you manage the unexpected on a regular basis. Once you manage a couple of presentation crises and realize you survived, you learn you can handle anything thrown your way in that arena too.

Do unexpected occurrences make us happy? Of course not. Can you still achieve your goal? Usually yes.

Remember—You're Not Alone

One last piece of advice about connecting with yourself: you don't have to do it alone. When you *are* tied up in your shorts, go ask a trusted colleague or team member for help. Ask for input on your content, feedback about what you're doing right, constructive feedback as you rehearse— whatever you need to get untangled. I've even been known to ask a colleague for a handshake or a hug before I go onstage to help calm my nerves. (In his book *Speaking Up without Freaking Out,* Matt Abrahams describes how to use oxytocin, a "bonding" hormone your body produces when you hug someone, shake hands, or kiss your significant other, to reduce your fear.)

Asking for help or reassurance does not make you any less competent; it just means you're human.

CHAPTER 3

Connect with Your Message

Empathize to optimize.

After dinner and a keynote at a National Speakers Association meeting, several of us stood around chatting. We'd been so engaged by the speaker that we continued discussing the topic long after the talk was over. As speakers, of course, we want people to remember us, so we began to reflect on what makes presentations memorable.

Tommy Hilcken, a motivational humorist, piped up that every time he speaks his goal is to be remarkable. "You know what it means to be remarkable?" he said. "That when you're done, people are remarking about what you just said!"

I thought that was pure brilliance. When you speak, if your goal is to connect and achieve, you must be remarkable. Your words must be memorable and repeatable.

How do you do that? By connecting with your message.

The Importance of Connecting with Your Message

Connecting with your message helps eliminate any doubt you might feel about what you're saying. When you're not confident in your message, the audience disengages and disregards what you say.

Additionally, from a practical standpoint, content drives delivery. If you are engaged and in the moment with your message, your delivery becomes easier. Bonus!

It may sound counterintuitive, but to connect with your message—to optimize it—you must empathize with your audience. That is, you must understand what is important to them and have the message reflect their issues and concerns. Empathize to optimize…

Don't Make Your Audience Think

In his book *Don't Make Me Think*, web-usability expert Steve Krug counsels against complicating things. He explains that online audiences are so fast-paced and so attuned to finding things easily, that if you make your website at all difficult to navigate, users will leave. Struggling to order a product? Go find it somewhere else. Can't find the contact information? Go hire someone else. Confused by the site organization? Don't have time to waste—bye-bye.

In the IT world, these kinds of problems are called "friction." Poor design gets in the way of doing business. When customers find too much friction—when it's too much work to do business with you—they take their business elsewhere.

I believe most of your listeners would agree with Krug's advice: Don't make them think. Your goal is to convey your message to your audience so they understand it and can take action as appropriate. Don't force them to figure out what you're saying.

Make your message as simple and as easy to follow as possible. This doesn't mean dumb it down; you may have a complex message to give. It does mean do everything in your power to clarify your message and organize the content to eliminate friction, which could include too much information, unnecessary information, disorganized information... Well, you get the idea.

Don't make them think.

Don't Just Get through It; Help Your Audience Get It

Have you ever been working on a presentation and thought, *Oh, I just have to get through this?* I know I have.

What that statement really means is that you're probably more concerned about your own needs than your audience's. That attitude will affect where you focus and how you craft your message. Your just-get-through-it attitude will come through, your messaging will suffer, and the audience will tune out. If you're not interested, why should they be interested?

To achieve business results in any presentation, you must commit to helping your audience "get it." To close that big deal, amp up the sales force, or get everyone on the same page for a new initiative, shift your focus to the audience. What do they need to get so that in return you achieve your goal?

The minute you commit to *getting it* rather than getting *through* it, your presentation approach becomes audience-centric. You start to consider who's there, why they are there, what they already know, and what they need to know. You begin to empathize with them so you can optimize your message for them. You naturally begin to explore new ways of engaging your listeners so they truly understand the importance of the topic at hand. Chances are you'll find yourself excited and engaged as well, and your presentation style will become more authentic.

As author Carmen Taran says, "If they can't repeat it, they didn't get it."

Turn Your Presentation into a Revelation

A Europe-based logistics company used a set slide for their quarterly financial discussions. It had a bar chart with sales by region and included years and years of data. It was just too much. I asked the president of the North American division to describe which elements were *critical* to the conversation. When we boiled it down to its core, he realized the takeaway message for this slide was that the automobile segment of the business used to be big and now was small. The company used to have huge market share, which now had shrunk. He changed the slide from a busy bar chart to an image of two cars, one large, one small. The image gave the executive team insight about the company's market position and focused their conversation on what to do about it.

The reason for giving a presentation rather than sending a report is because you—the speaker—add value. Or at least, you *should* add value. Your listeners want you to reveal something that they may not have seen on their own, just as the logistics division president did for the executive team.

When you step up to speak, present your topic in a way that provides a refreshingly new context: tell a story, share a little-known fact, or create an interesting metaphor. Make the data mean something. Show me how you interpret it with your deep expertise; tell me how I can use it. If you make your presentation a revelation, you can change how people think and how they respond to events. You can inspire action.

Ask yourself: *What do I want to reveal to my audience?*

Go for Intention, Not Precision

When you understand the true endgame is not your performance but rather the business results, you realize you can focus on the intention of your message rather than the precision of its words. Rather than memorizing a script, you can have a conversation with the audience. Rather than reading your slides so you don't forget a single point, you can glance at your confidence monitor[1] and grab the main ideas.

[1] A confidence monitor is a screen that faces the speaker. It displays what the audience sees, frequently with the upcoming slide and a countdown clock. It's often a fairly large display on the floor, but it could also be a small monitor on or near the lectern.

When you focus on precision, you get in your head. Go for intention instead. What's the gist of your message? What do you need to help your audience understand?

CHAPTER 4

Connect with Your Audience

Connection, not perfection.

The sales team was presenting to a major airline for a huge piece of business. Right off the bat they put themselves in their potential client's shoes. They flew on that airline to the corporate office. On the flight, they met the crew, chatted with them a bit, and took some photos.

When the first presenter got up to speak, he started off, "I want you to meet the crew who got us here to you." He showed the flight crew's pictures, said a little bit about each member, and described how well they took care of him and his team in getting them to town.

He continued, "And now I want to introduce you to *your* team, your crew—*us*—because our intention is to take just as good care of you."

The sales team listened to the potential client and demonstrated they understood the company's culture—they connected. They made the pitch. They got the business.

The Importance of Connecting with Your Audience

When most people hear the words "public speaking," their minds leap to delivery, to platform skills, to being in front of an audience. And that's when they panic.

Let me tell you a secret: by connecting with yourself and connecting with your message, 80% of your work is done. When you've made that investment, delivery is a piece of cake. You've done the work and set yourself up for success. Now it's all about connecting with your audience, which is what makes your message stick. It's what moves them to action. It's what inspires them to create change.

Without connection, it's hard to get the business results you need.

Remember It's Never about You; It's Always about Your Audience

Whether you're on a ballroom stage or in a conference room down the hall, the spotlight's on you. It feels like the presentation is all about You—after all, everyone's looking at You. It's enough to make the best of us self-conscious. *Am I doing this right? Do I look OK? Can they see me sweating? Am I remembering all my words?*

Know that you are in good company—we all get nervous—but make your listeners more important than any anxiety you experience. Keep the focus on how your message will benefit your audience (after all, you've optimized it for them). Doing so will redirect your thinking and your energy and help ensure success.

While you may be the speaker, your presentation is never about you; it's always about the audience.

Think the Thought

Kim, the vice president of marketing, was so concerned with her scripted performance that she forgot about her message. After a run-through, I asked her how it went for her, and then asked if she was open to some feedback. She nodded. I said, "You kinda sounded like a commercial." She blinked. "Did you just tell me I sounded like a commercial?" I smiled and responded, "Did I ever tell you I give clear and direct feedback?"

We laughed about it, and then went on to discuss what she was *thinking* as she was speaking. It turned out her mind was not on the words coming out of her mouth. She had the right facial expressions, right gestures, and right tone, but she didn't have personal engagement. And that's where audience disconnect happens.

Listeners know when you're mindlessly reciting your message. You come across as lifeless or superficial, because you're not thinking about what you're saying.

You must be fully engaged in your presentation or your listeners will tune out. To stay connected with your message *and* your audience, here is my million-dollar tip: *think the thought.*

What the heck does that even mean?

Picture reading a children's book aloud to a young audience. Do you *read* the story, or *tell* the story? Reading the story gets the words in the air. Telling the story engages the imagination. The young ones lean toward you in anticipation; they *experience* the story.

Thinking the thought is like telling the story. It keeps you personally engaged. In the moment of speaking, you are present to what you're saying. You catch yourself thinking, *That's not what I planned to say, but it worked—that's cool!* or *Oh, I just heard something in the prior session; let me bring it into the discussion.* You become pliable, and your message becomes pliable, because you're paying attention. You get it, and, as a result, your audience gets it. Since you stay engaged, your audience stays engaged.

There is one particular situation in which it's easy to disengage from your message, and I suspect many of us have faced it. When presentations have gone through a legal or compliance review, speakers often feel confined as to what they can say. But keep in mind it is usually the *slides* that have been through review, not *you*. You can still give context for the information on the slides. If you don't, you'll be bored, and your audience will know it. You must find something interesting. Ask yourself, *If legal review were out of the picture, how would I talk about this?* You might find it opens you up to new ideas and, trust me, your audience will appreciate it.

Think the thought.

Be Spontaneous

When presenting, take advantage of what's happening in real-time. Interact with your audience, acknowledge their presence, and be spontaneous. One of my favorite ways to be spontaneous is to throw in little-known facts (LKF) as they occur to me during my presentation. No, not random facts, but relevant items that come up in the moment because of the response from or interaction with the audience. I even write "LKF" on my script as a reminder. Tip: To be spontaneous like this, you have to be thinking the thought!

Go for Connection, Not Perfection

While discussed earlier, it's worth repeating: your audience is looking for connection, not perfection. They don't want facades; they don't want distance; they don't want walls. Your audience is not there to criticize or shoot arrows at you. They are not judge and jury.

Take that perfectionist pressure off yourself. If you connect with your audience in a meaningful way, they will forgive any mistakes, any signs of nervousness (remember Eddie who tripped going on stage?). Whenever you step up to speak, remember it's all about connection, not perfection. You don't have to be flawless; you do have to care.

To this point, we've been discussing the Talk on Water mindset, the differentiator that allows you to develop a powerhouse presentation, and with that the importance

of connection. A little philosophical, yes? Now let's shift
to a more strategic use of those foundational elements. In
Part 2 we look at how Presentation Profiling will shape your
success in each presentation.

PART TWO
Presentation Profiling

CHAPTER 5

Presentation Profiling Overview

What role are you playing—
Expert, Interpreter, or Catalyst?

Steve had just been promoted into the C-suite as the CFO of a Fortune 500 apparel company. Bright and capable, he knew that making presentations went along with his new position, but he felt unsure of himself and a bit awkward. He hired me to help him develop TED-like presentation skills for several upcoming presentations, including his quarterly financial report to the executive team.

As we worked on the financial presentation, I kept asking him questions like "What do those numbers mean? How does that data fit with this? How does this column relate to that?" My intent was to help him put the information in context to make it more meaningful to the executives.

We were making progress, but during one session Steve stopped me. "Time-out. I was just informed that for this quarterly report all I'm supposed to do is report the num-

bers on a prescribed template." That's all the executives
wanted: the numbers. While the request seemed odd to
both of us, that input allowed us to recalibrate to better
meet expectations. Steve realized his vision of stepping on
a stage and having to talk like TED wasn't required.

In that pivotal moment, I thought, *There must be an easier way... How can I help clients match what they must accomplish
to the skills needed for success? How can I help them understand their
presentation "job" so they deliver results?*

The Presentation Profiling Model

Reflecting on my years of experience, I noted several things.
First, presentations are not a one-size-fits-all proposition;
each presentation is unique. Different types of presentations
require different skills to be effective, and varying amounts
of time and effort to prepare. A main-stage presentation at
an industry event requires different preparation and skills
than an analyst summit does; going after new business
requires a different skill set than presenting market research
findings at an internal marketing meeting.

I also noted that speakers typically assume one of three
roles when delivering a presentation: someone sharing facts
and expertise, someone turning information into action, or
someone disrupting the status quo and painting a picture
of possibility. These observations evolved into the Presentation Profiling™ model, shown in Figure 1 as concentric
circles for three profiles—Expert, Interpreter, and Catalyst.

At the center is the Expert, whose purpose is to inform.
The Expert profile encompasses baseline concepts and

skills needed in all three roles. Next is the Interpreter, whose purpose is to influence. The Interpreter builds on the Expert profile and adds a clear call to action. Finally, the Catalyst's purpose is more visionary in nature—igniting change and disrupting the status quo. The arrow going out from the center of the circles illustrates how the time, effort, and skills required increase as the profile changes. Intuitively, you can see how delivering straightforward information (Expert) differs from painting a picture of dynamic cultural change (Catalyst).[2]

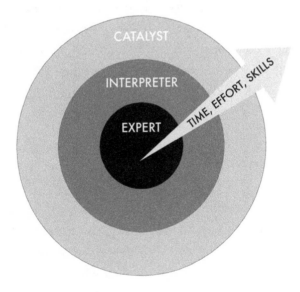

Figure 1: Presentation Profiling™ Model

[2] I also worked with Sharon McMillen Cannon, a professor at UNC's Kenan-Flagler Business School, to develop the Presentation Profiling™ assessment tool, a detailed questionnaire that helps speakers clarify their role as well as assess the skills needed to perform it effectively.

Before we get into more depth on each role, notice your reaction to the words Expert, Interpreter, and Catalyst. Your initial reaction to Expert might be "Ho-hum, I expect to be bored." When you hear Interpreter you may think word-for-word translation. Or you may expect a Catalyst to be a dynamic, motivational, inspirational, rally-the-troops speaker. Please recognize—and this is important—that "Expert" is not synonymous with "boring." All speakers, Experts included, can and should generate curiosity so their listeners want to pay attention. Interpreters are indeed bilingual, but in a broader sense. They put information in context and turn it into action; they also translate action-oriented messages up and down the chain of command. And while indeed a Catalyst should be inspirational, any of the profiles can and should inspire. One profile is not better than the others—all are important and needed.

Benefits of Presentation Profiling

Using these profiles with clients offers two huge benefits. First, it increases connection. Because presenters understand what they're being asked to do—their purpose—they're better able to connect with themselves, which in turn helps them connect with their message and their audience. Second, these profiles become internal shorthand. One client exclaimed, "You mean I can tell someone it's an Expert or Interpreter presentation and they'll understand the expectations? That makes my job easier!"

Our CFO, Steve, was being asked to be an Expert. While perhaps unexpected, gaining that clarity simplified his preparation. As you read this part of the book, look for signs of "Ah, *that's* the profile I need to take on for this presentation." I should note, Presentation Profiling is not a personality test—it's not trying to label who *you* are. It's a tool to determine what needs to be accomplished and what it will take to be successful for a specific presentation. You may change profiles from speech to speech; you may also find you use one profile more frequently than the others.

When you effectively take on the role of an Expert, an Interpreter, or a Catalyst, the preparation and delivery of your speech becomes clearer. *This role clarity is a differentiator for a powerhouse presentation.*

CHAPTER 6

The Expert

Informing with interest.

My husband, John, needed surgery on his C5-C6-C7 vertebrae. The procedure would take place close to his brain, entailing significant risk of nerve damage or other severe side effects. We interviewed four surgeons; he narrowed it down to two, then debated between them.

"Well, I know who I'd go with," I said.

"Who?" he asked.

"The last doctor," I said.

"Why?"

"Because in less than a minute, he explained the procedure and I understood it. After the surgery, I feel like I could have a conversation with him and understand your recovery—or any issues that come up."

This surgeon demonstrated complete expertise. He didn't try to influence me. He just educated me, and he did it clearly and with empathy. It was obvious I wasn't the first family member he'd explained the delicate procedure to. He understood my fears and concerns and the questions I was likely to have.

I'm happy to report the surgery went as planned. The doctor came to speak with me immediately following the surgery; he continued to use plain English and my questions were easily answered. His communication skills boosted my confidence about John's recovery. While I may not need this physician's services in the future, because of his communication abilities, I wouldn't hesitate to recommend him.

Wouldn't you like a similar result from your business presentations?

The Expert's Endgame

My guess is that you don't have to explain complicated medical procedures on a daily basis. More likely you are told something like "We need you to discuss the second-quarter performance in no more than four slides."

As an Expert, your goal is to efficiently communicate facts and share information about a given subject; you aren't necessarily invested in what listeners do with the information they receive. In other words, you need to perform a mind-meld with your audience—take the information in your head and put it into their head. Once it's there, the recipient can decide what to do with it.

You may find yourself using the Expert profile in situations such as:

- A product launch – Your marketing team shares information with the sales team—market research findings, the campaign collateral strategy, the top ten ways the company outperforms the competition. You give the sales team valuable context and positioning, but they determine how to deliver the information to their prospects.

- A status report – As the program director, you keep the executive team informed of progress, issues, and next steps, but no action is needed.

- Research findings – As principal scientist, you present your latest research at a conference; it's up to the listeners to decide whether they should do anything with it.

You may have been asked to speak because of your deep domain knowledge, but you don't have to be a technical person or a scientist to be an Expert. "Expert" simply means your goal is to provide information.

The Effective Expert

We've talked about mindset and connecting with yourself, your message, and your audience. All those things apply to each of the three presentation profiles. However, there are a few refinements worth highlighting for the Expert profile.

(Since the Expert is the baseline profile, these strategies apply to the other profiles as well.)

ADD VALUE BEYOND A REPORT

Because an Expert provides information without having a specific action-oriented outcome, you might wonder, *Can't I just send a report?* Good question. Sometimes a report will do the trick—and may be preferred for timeliness and expense.

However, when you *are* asked to give a presentation, the onus is on you to make sure you offer more than a written report can. Your goal is to provide value for your listeners by giving them what they need in a way they can easily understand. What unique insights do you have? What backstory can you give that enlightens the listeners? As discussed earlier, what can you reveal to your audience? Your perspective adds value.

ADJUST YOUR LANGUAGE TO YOUR AUDIENCE

In an ideal Expert environment, you get to speak to others in your field, so you can use technical jargon and go spelunking into details. While occasionally you find this scenario in business, more often you'll have an audience with different levels of interest and understanding. You'll probably need to use less detail and plainer lay language. Tip: Comparisons, metaphors, and analogies help explain unfamiliar concepts in familiar terms.

Know who's in your audience and why they're there so you can give them what they need in a language they understand.

FOCUS YOUR CONTENT

It's tempting for Experts to want to do a data dump. "Hey, I can give them AAAAALL the information, and *they* can figure out what's important!" Nope. We need more finesse than that. The information you provide must be *meaningful*.

In essence, you're teaching the audience something, so you have to think about what information is provided and how it's provided *from the learner's point of view*. If you give students everything, how can they possibly know what to pay attention to? We all have only a limited amount of mental real estate...

The Expert's Top 3 Traps

When you use the Expert profile, you are providing information that typically is within your domain of expertise. Your knowledge, experience, and perspective can be of great value to listeners; however, many experts often know so much that it impedes their communication. When you use the Expert profile, pay special attention to the following traps. (And not to belabor the point, but these traps can catch Interpreters and Catalysts as well.)

TRAP #1: INFORMATION OVERLOAD

If you hear a speaker say, "I know this is a lot of information, but..." or "I know you can't read this slide, but let me tell you what it says...," you're probably experiencing information overload, affectionately known as drinking from the fire hose. If you hear *yourself* saying one of these things, look out! You're probably spraying your listeners with way too much information.

In an effort to be complete, Experts often feel obligated to share every single thing they know rather than considering just what listeners absolutely need to know. Like the Energizer Bunny they keep going...and going...and going... and as a result, the now-overwhelmed audience forgets most of it.

Rather than think, *Aack! I've got thirty minutes—how am I going to fill it?* think, *I have thirty minutes. What can I reasonably cover in that amount of time?* Rather than provide a laundry list of information, *curate* what you give your audience. They will trust they can come to you for more information when needed.

TRAP #2: THE CURSE OF KNOWLEDGE

You know how to tie your shoes. You've been doing it for years; it's second nature. However, if you need to teach a four-year-old how to tie her shoes, chances are you will struggle to explain it. This is the "curse of knowledge" explained so well by Chip Heath and Dan Heath in their book *Made to Stick*—that cognitive state where you know something so well that you cannot remember what it's like to *not* know it—you take the knowledge for granted.[3]

Another example: Have you ever asked an attorney to explain what a tort is? The last time I did, the attorney used

---

3 This concept was first articulated by Camerer, Loewenstein, and Weber in the *Journal of Political Economy* in 1989.

a whole lot of words without saying anything I could understand. The tort was so foundational to his knowledge that he couldn't explain it.

Experts get caught in the curse of knowledge regularly. They jump in too deep, too fast without offering enough context for their listeners to keep up. They skip something foundational (like the definition of tort), and as a result, little sticks.

To avoid the curse of knowledge, you must understand your audience. What do your listeners *need* to know, what do they *want* to know, and what do they *already* know? Go back to the beginning; pretend you're hearing this information for the first time. What's foundational? If possible, talk to some audience members so you learn what level of understanding they already have. When possible, test your draft presentation with someone from your audience—or at least test it with someone who is *not* an expert in the topic.

TRAP #3: MISTAKING CONTENT ISSUES FOR DELIVERY PROBLEMS

If you get audience feedback that you use filler words, move aimlessly, and stand with poor posture, you may have an underlying problem: poor content. If you don't clarify your message and organize your content appropriately, you are left relying on your delivery skills. And if your content doesn't engage your audience, all they experience is your delivery. If they don't engage in your content, they'll engage in criticizing those nuisance habits we all have...

With an Expert, the content tends to get more complicated than it needs to be. Focus on clarifying and simplifying your content. Your audience will understand the message more easily and, as a bonus, your delivery will come more easily.

When using the Expert profile, trust that you know your stuff—you've got the domain expertise. Focus on bringing your knowledge to the audience in a way they can grasp. Once they get it, they can decide how to leverage it and what, if anything, they should do next.

EXPERTS, ASK YOURSELVES:

- [ ] What am I providing that my audience won't get from reading a report?
- [ ] What does my audience absolutely need to know?
- [ ] What does my audience already know?
- [ ] What is the core message I need people to take away?
- [ ] Have I provided enough information without including too many details?

CHAPTER 7

The Interpreter

Translating for action.

Rufus was an associate director who prided himself on his expertise and precision, and indeed his colleagues valued his deep knowledge. However, for Rufus to get promoted to full director, he needed to demonstrate a different awareness, to offer a different voice at the table. He needed to show broader perspective and speak to strategy rather than execution.

Knowing this context, Rufus and I worked on his presentation to senior leadership about a proposed employee benefits strategy. Because he needed their buy-in, one of my first questions was "Who have you consulted with?" As a subject-matter expert, Rufus held the belief that he needed to do everything himself. He hadn't thought of asking for input or feedback. My next questions: "Who will be resistant? Why? Do you understand their perspective?

How can you include them and maybe win them over ahead of time?"

Just hearing these questions broadened Rufus's thinking. He realized the value of asking for input and understanding various points of view before he spoke. He was able to learn the executives' perspectives, respond to them in advance, and incorporate relevant information into his presentation.

As it happened, Rufus did *not* achieve the desired approval of the proposed strategy, at least not immediately. However, because he'd learned new influencing skills, the executives' perception of him changed. They began to speak about him differently—and he did get his promotion.

The Interpreter's Endgame

As an Expert, you provide data and give analysis; you may even tell stories and use metaphors, all with the goal of sharing information. When you move to the Interpreter profile, you do all those same things, and also add a **specific call to action.** As an Interpreter, you need the audience to *act*.

But a call to action can't just be tagged on at the end of your speech. ("Here's a bunch of numbers—and oh, by the way, can you cut your budget 10% please?" Uh, no.) Asking for action requires translating information into insight and offering it in a way that creates meaning and implications for the audience. Your listeners must understand *what* you're asking and *why* you're asking for it.

You may have found yourself playing the Interpreter role in these types of situations:

- Making a sales pitch – The call to action for almost any salesperson is "Buy our products!" or "Choose our services!" (though perhaps with a bit more finesse).

- Asking for investors – A start-up's executive team may ask venture capitalists to invest in their business idea; an established company may hold an IPO.

- Advocating for a policy – Businesses, lobbyists, action groups, and individuals regularly advocate for regulators to change or retain a particular policy.

However, the everyday example of an Interpreter is the mid-level manager who takes information from the shop floor and interprets it for upper management, or who takes strategy from the C-suite and translates it for the front line. (I'd be willing to bet most of you are nodding your head right now recognizing the value of a good translator.)

Influencing people to act is what gets things done.

The Effective Interpreter

As an Interpreter, it's important to convey information but *critical* you connect with the audience and gain buy-in. Several specific strategies can help.

BECOME BILINGUAL

Interpreters are bilingual or multilingual. In presenting, you might not literally need to speak more than one language, but figuratively you do. We already mentioned how an Interpreter needs to translate information into insights and meaning. You may also need to translate between technical gurus and lay people, between the finance department and VPs.

If you can't put information into words your audience will understand, how can they take action? Get to know the language they speak, so you don't leave them guessing what you mean.

ATTUNE TO THE AUDIENCE

Besides speaking your listeners' language, your ability to influence them depends on your ability to get inside their head, understand the issue from their perspective, and see the world through their eyes. Don't dismiss your own opinions, beliefs, or theories; do be curious and willing to familiarize yourself with the topic or situation from your listeners' perspective. Additionally, consider how your audience views *you*, as that perception can impact how a message is heard.

BUILD THE BUSINESS CASE

You need your listeners to *do* something—you need them to take action. Help them understand *why* they should take action. Build a strong business case throughout your talk.

Ask yourself:

- What specific action needs to be taken?
- What does your audience need to *know and understand* to take action?
- *Why* do they need to take the action?
- What happens *if they don't?*

The Interpreter's Top 3 Traps

Since Interpreters' purpose is to move an audience into action, they tend to get tripped up in areas related to their relationship with that audience. Pay attention to the following traps (and recognize Catalysts can get caught in some of them too).

TRAP #1: HAVING THE WRONG PEOPLE IN THE ROOM

You know what action is needed, but do you have the right people in the room—the ones who can make it happen? If you spend your energy with an audience without the authority to act, it doesn't matter how well you speak; you will fail.

For example, during executive meetings at a health network, the nurses were assigned various actions, but the nurses never followed through. The problem? No one was bringing the nurses' input to the discussion. They were being given expectations that were impossible to accomplish within the given protocols.

Make sure your call to action and your audience are aligned. Talk to the people who can make the change you need.

TRAP #2: THINKING THE PRESENTATION IS THE ENDGAME

One of the Interpreter's chief jobs is to anticipate resistance and gain buy-in. This does not magically occur when you stand up to speak. (Surprise!) Just because you request, tell, or even demand some action doesn't mean it will get done.

Your presentation is only one step in the process—it just happens to be the most public step. The rest of the process entails talking in advance with the people who can influence the outcome so you understand their perspective, identify their concerns and objections, and can adapt your message. The conversation may even need to continue after your presentation, so you can reinforce your message and the need for action. Your presentation is not the endgame; the business goal—the action needed—is the endgame.

TRAP #3: TRYING TO MAKE THE AUDIENCE MOVE TOO FAST

When you develop a presentation, you become steeped in the topic. You understand the details, you understand the rationale, you see clearly why the company needs to move from Point A to Point B. Your audience, on the other hand, may be hearing this information for the first time. If you ask them for a large leap rather than a small step, they may balk.

Take yourself back in time to your initial exploration of this change. That's where your audience is. Start there

with them and take them in small steps toward the understanding they need to take the action you want. What feels
like a baby step to you may be a quantum leap for your
listeners.

When using the Interpreter profile, go beyond simply
getting your audience to understand—help them recognize
the need to take action. The ability to translate a message
from an informative presentation to a call to action is what
sets the Interpreter apart.

INTERPRETERS, ASK YOURSELVES:

☐ What is my call to action?

☐ Where is my audience now, and where do they need to be?

☐ Is my audience open, skeptical, or split on the issue?

☐ What common ground do different groups of listeners share?

☐ What common ground do I share with listeners?

☐ What stories, metaphors, & comparisons help convey my message?

☐ What's my business case for them to take action?

☐ Have I prepared enough to be conversational and to connect?

CHAPTER 8

The Catalyst

Disrupting the status quo; envisioning tomorrow.

NJ Sharing Network is responsible for recovery and placement of donated organs and tissue for the nearly 4,000 New Jersey residents in need of a lifesaving transplant. They're also part of the national system to support 115,000 people on the transplant waiting list across the U.S. Their cause is one near and dear to my heart. Having worked with them since 2012, I've seen up close that it's not just what they do but how they do it that makes a difference. They've succeeded at painting a picture of organ and tissue donation that has changed how people view it. As a result, NJ Sharing Network has grown in every way possible— including philanthropic support, number of volunteers, and families served.

One of the primary catalysts for this success is Elisse, the vice president and chief administrative officer of the organization and the executive director of its foundation. She joined the foundation as an experienced development expert and quickly started growing its philanthropic base. But things really shifted when she started bringing more than just the numbers into the boardroom and into the broader public conversation. By focusing on *why* they do what they do and the benefit to all involved, Elisse and NJ Sharing Network have captured people's hearts.

They make the extent of the need concrete:

- Imagine the number of people you could fit in MetLife Stadium in New Jersey (82,500)—the national waiting list is 40% more people than that.

- Of the people who register to donate, only 1% actually qualify when they die, due to cause of death or other medical issues.

- Just one donor can save eight lives and enhance the lives of more than fifty people through tissue donation.

Then they put a human face on the need. They share stories about people whose lives were saved by organ donation and the impact on their families—including many of the employees who have been touched directly. They describe the rituals they use to honor the donors and the impact on the donor families; they honor everyone involved in the process.

By envisioning a future where 115,000 people no longer have to wait for transplants, NJ Sharing Network has inspired people to become followers and supporters and volunteers. The vision has created so much passion that it's taken on a life of its own—from growth in the number of locations for the annual 5K fundraising race to the employees' creation of a meditation garden to honor donor families.

One person alone cannot create change, but one person can act as a catalyst for change. Elisse's approach to communicating NJ Sharing Network's message created a movement. In fact, longtime colleagues now refer to the organization's historical periods as "BE" and "AE"—before Elisse and after Elisse.

Now *that's* a Catalyst.

The Catalyst's Endgame

When you're a Catalyst, your role is to spark change. You move beyond the specific call to action of an Interpreter and paint a picture of possibility, disrupting your listeners' current view of the world and igniting their imagination—without necessarily telling them how to achieve that vision. As a Catalyst, you encourage listeners to believe in a different future and in their ability to contribute to change. Sounds grandiose, doesn't it?

Even the examples that come to mind for Catalyst presentations can intimidate:

- Political speeches – President John F. Kennedy set a goal of putting a man on the moon and getting him safely back, but he didn't tell the engineers how to do it.

- Product launches – Apple cofounder Steve Jobs told us to invent tomorrow, but he didn't say exactly how we should get there. (He did, however, demonstrate by giving us iDevices we didn't even know we needed.)

- TED Talks – Facebook COO Sheryl Sandberg encourages us (women, in particular) to "lean in," to break societal and personal barriers, but she can't tell each of us specifically what to do.

Despite the iconic examples above, you don't have to be famous to be a Catalyst. You may be a business leader who believes passionately that changing the status quo is not only possible but absolutely necessary to grow, expand, or revive your company. You may be a nonprofit leader with a vision of making the world a better place. You may be a volunteer board member compelled to kindle innovation and generate fresh ideas. A Catalyst is any leader whose mission is to create broader change and move people toward the future.

Sometimes we hear "catalyst" and think "motivational speaker." Let's get the troops revved up! A one-shot motivational speaker may indeed catalyze new ideas and rev up the audience, but in the business world a Catalyst often has to play a longer game. While you certainly find leaders giving Catalyst presentations in companies known as innovators and disruptors, many businesses need Catalysts because if they don't change—if they become stale or stagnant—they run the risk of decline. This type of cultural change doesn't come from one motivational speech; it requires consistent messaging over time—both on and off stage.

A true Catalyst in business presentations is less common than you might think. More frequently, the Interpreter profile is indicated. Do you need to make a specific call to action? Use the Interpreter profile. Are you trying to change the world or disrupt the status quo, painting a picture of the future and asking for more general movement? Hello, Catalyst!

The Effective Catalyst

The most effective Catalysts are driven by a deep passion and sense of purpose, which can't necessarily be taught. But if the Catalyst profile is indicated for your presentation, here are a few pieces of advice.

LIVE UP TO THE NAME

I've said more than once that a presentation is a conversation with your audience. The skills you need to talk to friends at dinner are the same ones you need on stage—just bigger. Giving a Catalyst presentation is one of those places where bigger might need to be even BIGGER.

Of the three profiles, the Catalyst typically requires the most advanced presentation delivery skills. While you still need to be authentic both on stage and off, you may need to push yourself to develop a more dynamic persona on stage. You don't have to go pro as a motivational speaker, but you might *feel* like one as you stretch your boundaries to spread your message.

BE REAL

As a Catalyst you're urging listeners to move outside their comfort zone. To be willing to do that, they must trust you. Building trust requires that you demonstrate consistency, authenticity, and even vulnerability.

Be transparent. Share your feelings. What motivates you? Why is this change so important? What will be the impact of this disruption? What will it accomplish for the organization, or for the greater good? How will the organization feel, or how will the enterprise be different when the goal is realized? Openness demonstrates your passion and builds trust. Be real.

COMMIT TO COLLABORATION

Despite our unbounded dreams as idealistic youth, we've learned we can't change the world alone. Effective Catalysts recognize that results happen through collaboration, and they commit to engaging listeners in the conversation.

Have you seen Derek Sivers's TED Talk "How to Start a Movement"? He shows a fantastically entertaining video of a guy dancing on a grassy hill in public and proceeds to analyze what it takes "dancing guy" to get his first follower, then additional followers until, finally, the dancing becomes a movement. (My favorite quote: "The first follower is what transforms a lone nut into a leader.")

As a Catalyst, you want and need the audience to say, "Let's do it!" Value their contribution.

The Catalyst's Top 3 Traps

Catalysts see the future clearly, but they can get so wrapped up in the vision that they lose people along the way. Once you've made sure that the Catalyst profile is truly the one needed, avoid the following pitfalls so you can keep people with you.

TRAP #1: BUILDING CASTLES IN THE AIR

If you don't give your audience something tangible to hold on to, your visions become daydreams that fade as soon as you're done speaking. While you may not need to include specific steps to reach the desired outcome, you do need to speak in concrete language and with specific examples that help your audience relate to your big idea.

TRAP #2: HAVING A THIN SKIN

When you're a Catalyst, you're a change agent, and humans don't like change. (Surprise!) Not everyone will like what you say; you will encounter opposing points of view. If your message is particularly disruptive, you may even get arrows in the back. Develop a thick skin and be ready for backlash.

TRAP #3: GETTING CAUGHT IN EGO

There's a bit of romance associated with the idea of being a Catalyst. Since you often speak from a place of personal power, it can be tempting to allow others to put you on a pedestal. As a result, it may appear you talk down to people.

Instead, consider the concept of servant leadership. While an age-old philosophy, the modern description comes from Robert Greenleaf, who describes it thus: "The servant-leader is servant first... It begins with the natural feeling that one wants to serve, to serve first. Then conscious choice brings one to aspire to lead."

The most effective Catalysts serve a higher purpose, a greater good; they connect authentically, even humbly.

When using the Catalyst profile, you're working with transformative ideas that have the potential to make a significant difference. Focus on painting a picture that sparks innovation and ignites change.

CATALYSTS, ASK YOURSELVES:

- [ ] Does this message reflect my passion and conviction?
- [ ] What can I do to help the audience understand the issues?
- [ ] How can I paint a vision of what could be?
- [ ] Is my message clear and relatable to all my listeners?
- [ ] How will I break through emotional barriers with disruptive content?
- [ ] Does my delivery come across as transparent and authentic?
- [ ] Do I offer a perspective that encourages others to join in?

PART THREE

The Presentation C.O.D.E.

CHAPTER 9

C.O.D.E. Overview

"Don't make me think."

Now that you're aware of the Talk on Water mindset and understand the importance of connection (Part 1), and you've determined the appropriate presentation profile— Expert, Interpreter, or Catalyst (Part 2)—take a deep breath. It's time to crack the presentation C.O.D.E.®, a simple four-step process to ensure you deliver a powerhouse presentation. We'll look at a quick overview of the strategy here, and then dig into the how-to's in the following chapters.

The first three steps cover content creation: *clarifying* your message, *organizing* the content, and maximizing the impact of your message by *developing* relevant slides or other forms of media. Once your content is solid, you can *express* yourself with conviction and *engage* your audience.

Step 1: Clarify Your Core Message

In Step 1, you gather information needed to identify and clarify your **core message,** a.k.a. your **unique perspective**. Your goal is to develop one simple sentence or phrase that clearly summarizes the essence of your presentation, providing focus and differentiating your story from others'.

By understanding who your audience is, why they care about the topic, and what they need to know to achieve results, you now have what you need to answer the question *what.* "If my audience takes away one key idea, *what* does it need to be?" Your unique perspective should be so simple that every person who leaves your presentation can repeat it—thus ensuring they got it.

Step 2: Organize Your Content

In Step 2, you answer the question *how.* "*How* am I going to talk about and support my core message in a way that will make sense to my listeners?" You do this by grouping your content into digestible bits of information with a logical structure, making sure everything maps back to your core message. Your goal is a presentation framework that allows listeners to quickly and easily understand the message. Then you put it all together with a compelling open and memorable close.

Remember your audience's perspective: "Don't make me think!" When you organize effectively, you optimize your listeners' ability to absorb the information, leverage the content, and act.

Step 3: Develop Your Audiovisuals

Once you've clarified and organized your information, it's time to consider whether to incorporate any media and, if so, the best way to do it. In Step 3, you develop audiovisual support to help your audience more quickly grasp what's being discussed. Specifically, this chapter describes how to design slide decks using the Glance & Grab strategy and RSVP principles.

When done right, your media supports rather than overpowers your presentation, and your audience can learn more in less time.

Step 4: Express Yourself & Engage Your Audience

Too many presenters adopt an artificial style or imitate someone notable, but in Step 4 your goal is to succeed at being *you*. When you express yourself with ease, energy, and enthusiasm, you project a self-assured confidence. Additionally, when you adeptly facilitate Q&A, you engage your audience even more effectively. Your authenticity results in a memorable presentation.

For ease of explanation, the C.O.D.E. process is described as linear; however, please recognize it's actually iterative. Here's what often happens: You begin with Clarify and then move to Organize, where you learn something new and have to go back to Clarify...then you're on to Organize again, then to Develop...and you realize something else so you go back to Clarify and Organize...then to Develop again and finally on to Express and Engage...and even *then* you backtrack once or twice! Don't let this iteration throw you—it is completely normal and expected. I promise, you will reach the end.

By using the C.O.D.E. process, you will truly own your message and talk on water. When you're sincere and authentic, your audience can't help but share your enthusiasm.

CHAPTER 10

Clarify Your Core Message

Be remarkable.

In a coaching session, eight business leaders were each developing a fifteen-minute presentation about a success story in which they had played a key role. These presentations would be delivered at an internal leadership conference to share lessons learned and inspire listeners to create their own success stories. For many of the presenters, this would be a defining moment in their career.

Yet as I listened to them practice, all the stories sounded the same. None of these presentations offered anything remotely memorable. I could have been anyone, anywhere, listening to a briefing on just about any business case. Every participant described in detail the project, what it took to do it, the results, and the lessons he or she had learned. In placing such an emphasis on the facts, each presenter failed to capture the essence of what made their story unique and therefore memorable to the audience.

When the speakers finished their run-through, we started digging deeper. I asked them questions like:

- What made this project successful?
- What went wrong (that dirty little secret)?
- Who was on the team? Why?
- What got you excited about this project?
- Why do you remember this story? What makes it remarkable?

At first, they were baffled. But they soon came to realize that their presentations were not having the desired effect. As they kept going deeper with their answers, they realized they had distinct perspectives that made their stories much more compelling. We moved from "Our project was a success" to "Lean processes made our employees' jobs easier and our customers happier" and "Frontline staff spoke truth to power, and management listened" and "Transparency let us address critical issues."

And *that* gave the audience something new to hang onto with each presentation, a real takeaway message. As a result, the presenters provided actionable insights and got a positive, dynamic reaction from their listeners.

What Is Your Core Message?

A **core message** is one simple sentence that clearly summarizes the essence of your presentation. It provides focus. In college when you were writing a paper, it was your thesis statement. In science, it's your hypothesis. In presentations, it's sometimes also referred to as a takeaway message. That one simple sentence allows your audience to "get it," to remember the gist of the presentation, and to take whatever action is needed. *This is a differentiator for a powerhouse presentation.*

Your core message clearly identifies what you want to accomplish in your presentation. Each of the three presentation profiles has a foundational purpose, which of course you make specific to your topic.

As an Expert, your purpose is to inform, for example, explaining a new process, giving a status report, or presenting findings. Your core message is related to what you want your audience to *know*.

As an Interpreter, you want to influence your listeners to do something. There's always a call to action, such as a recommendation to develop a new product, adopt a new marketing strategy, or pursue an acquisition. Your core message is related to what you want your audience to *do*.

As a Catalyst, you want to disrupt the status quo, generate new ideas, and create the space for new possibilities, for example, painting a picture of where the company will be in five years as a result of the new corporate strategy. Your core message is related to what you want your audience to *envision*.

Without a core message, your audience will be left wondering, "What am I supposed to know?" or "What am I supposed to do?" or "So what?"—and that's if they didn't check out during the talk. If your audience leaves not knowing what's important, you've wasted their time and yours. Whether Expert, Interpreter, or Catalyst, you have an endgame. Your core message drives you and your audience to that endgame.

Understanding Your Audience

To find your core message, start by researching your audience. Consider these questions:

- Who is your audience?
- Why is your audience there?
- What does your audience need to know?

WHO IS YOUR AUDIENCE?

When asked the question "Who is your audience?" many people answer with demographic information. "The board of directors." "The management team." "Decision makers." "Front-line, client-facing staff." "The attendees at an insurance conference." "Female customers age 40 to 60." Roles, ages, genders, decision-making authority.

Demographics are important, but when giving a business presentation with a specific purpose, it's often more important to understand how your listeners think, what their perspective is, and what beliefs they hold. You want to know about anything that might get in the way of your message being heard.

For example, when I gathered feedback on my client Michelle, colleagues described her as a consummate Expert, deeply knowledgeable in her subject. But Michelle's leadership team made it clear that if she wanted to be promoted to senior director, she had to be able to develop her Interpreter skills, influencing others to take action. While working on her presentation content, she realized her audience included people who were 1) setting the direction for the sales force, and 2) likely to be resistant to her ideas. That information provided great insight on how to talk to them.

Start with demographics but go further. "Who" is about understanding how people think and what they feel. Discover who is *really* going to be in the room.

WHY IS YOUR AUDIENCE THERE?

Once you've identified your audience, it's time to ask "Why are they here?" There might be more possibilities than you realize...

- They are interested in the subject. ("Oh, looks like an interesting breakout session.")

- They are decision makers who need your information. ("Should we choose this provider, or go with one of the others on the short list?")

- They felt obligated. ("It's mandatory.")

- They are advocates there to support the effort. ("I want to make sure the senior team is well represented; this is an important project.")

Don't assume. Don't make stuff up. Do your best to find out why your audience is there.

For example, if you're part of an investor relations team preparing for a high-stakes investor day at the New

York Stock Exchange, assess your audience: Who will be attending in person, who will be listening on a webcast, and who will be reading the transcript months from now? The obvious answer is a mix of sell-side analysts and buy-side investors. But dig deeper for some less obvious answers: *Why* are they plugged in? What's on their minds? What information do they need to hear and understand to form a position or make an investment decision? Peel back the layers of how your company is perceived by key stakeholders so you can create content that is truly on target.

Understanding your listeners' *why* helps you better prepare your content to address their needs and concerns.

WHAT DOES YOUR AUDIENCE NEED TO KNOW?

Given the information you have about who your audience is and why they're there, what do they absolutely need to know? To get your listeners to your objective, what do you need to communicate to them?

The easiest way to find out? Ask them.

For business presentations, you're frequently speaking to colleagues. If they must listen to you, they have a vested interest in helping you provide pertinent information. Have a water-cooler conversation with a couple of folks who will be in attendance. That may provide enough insight for many internal presentations.

For the highest-stakes presentations, you'll want to find out as much as you can about the audience. If possible, talk with a few people who will be attending your presentation. Ask questions such as:

- What is your experience and/or level of knowledge with this subject?

- What questions do you want answered?

- What are your concerns?

- What would make this presentation a good use of your time?

If you can't get to audience members themselves, talk to someone who knows that audience or has presented to them before. Talking to the board of directors? Ask the CEO who will be there what questions the board might have. Talking to the distribution team? Ask the sales director what will be most useful. Speaking at an industry conference? Ask your conference contact who the attendees are and which sessions they've found most beneficial in the past. Ask questions such as:

- What can you tell me about the audience? What do I need to know that I might not already know about them?

- If it's the first time the audience is hearing this topic, what do I need to make sure to tell them?

- What do they already know that I might need to remind them of?

- Are they able to discuss advanced information, or do I need to start with the basics?

Identify inaccurate assumptions. Many presenters get tripped up on inaccurate assumptions—whether their listeners' or their own.

As you speak with stakeholders to prepare, keep an eye out for these faulty assumptions. Listen carefully to what people say and don't say; try to understand the filter they're looking through. They may have misconceptions or inaccurate information. If you can clear up the misconceptions, it can help align audience members' interests with your endgame.

Proper preparation is the key to avoiding getting caught in faulty assumptions. Do your research and make sure your facts are correct.

Look for common ground. Whenever you speak, you are in the moving business. It is your job to move listeners from Point A to Point B as clearly and directly as possible. When you invest the effort to ask questions and understand their perspective, you are standing with your audience at Point A—you begin the journey with them on common ground.

Finding common ground among different audience segments will allow you to craft a core message that speaks to your entire audience. Each listener will feel that you understand him or her. As you organize and develop your talk, you'll be able to choose stories, metaphors, and language that everyone can relate to. At first glance, finding common ground may seem impossible, but there is always something your listeners have in common. It may take work to find it, but the payoff is worth it when a high-stakes presentation resonates with your *entire* audience.

Crafting Your Core Message

Once you've determined who your audience is and what they need to know, it's time to tackle crafting your core message. This is one of those tasks that is simple, but not easy. We often get so wrapped up in wanting to convey everything we know that it's difficult to identify the one overarching message we want the audience to remember.

During that coaching session with the eight leaders, I realized that the key to finding your core message was to find your unique perspective. Since then, I've come to use "core message" and "unique perspective" synonymously, because having that unique element is so critical. Your single sentence not only distills your entire talk, it distinguishes your message from everyone else's. Finding a core message can be messy, but *having a core message truly is a differentiator for a powerhouse presentation.*

HOW TO DEVELOP YOUR CORE MESSAGE

Let's get methodical. In this section we'll go through a series of questions to help distill your core message. Responses for a sample business scenario are provided so you can see the progression of answers from basic information to draft core message to final core message.

First, keeping in mind what you already know about your audience, answer these questions:

- What about this topic do you find interesting?

- What makes your interpretation unique?

- What about this topic will be of interest to
  your listeners?

*I'm working on a presentation about the new quality as-
surance approach we're implementing in IT. I was surprised to learn how much recoding we do because we wait
to test our software until near the end of the development
process. Just last year it cost us tens of thousands of dol-
lars in overtime to avoid delayed software deliveries, not
to mention the opportunity cost of the rework—all because
we test on the backend.*

*What makes my perspective unique is that I've been a
consultant and have seen how other companies do it. One
of the most efficient and effective ways to ensure quality is
to start testing right from the beginning rather than waiting for the end—it's the difference between driving quality
proactively and constantly chasing it with bug report after
bug report.*

*I think my listeners will be interested in this because if we
spend less time fixing errors, we have more time for new
projects. Plus, we get happier customers.*

Next, give some thought to the following:

- If my audience doesn't recall anything else,
  what one single thought do I want them to
  remember?

- By the end of this presentation, what do I want
  my audience to know/do/feel?

I want my audience to remember that if we use this new process, our quality will be higher, and we'll be more efficient. With the saved time, we can do more for our customers.

Now, can you encapsulate that into one sentence?

By implementing a new quality assurance process, instead of trying to get quality on the backend, we'll build it in from the beginning, which will make us more efficient and our customers happier.

Good attempt, but it's a little clunky. To keep your message as succinct as possible, think *simple.*

By implementing a new quality assurance process, we'll build in quality from the start.

Better. Depending on style, you could get even pithier.

We will drive quality rather than chase it.

Aha! If someone had to leave the room while you were speaking and afterward asked a colleague what you said, imagine if they heard, "She told us how we're going to drive quality from the beginning rather than chase it on the backend." Perfect! Without getting into the details of the quality assurance and testing process, the sentence encapsulates your talk.

Finding and clarifying your core message takes time and iteration. As you move through the next steps of the C.O.D.E. process (Organize, Develop, and Express), you'll keep refining your message. That's perfectly normal and expected. Throughout the iterations, just keep focusing on answering this question: "If my audience takes away just one key idea, what does it need to be?" Keeping it simple and clear makes it (and you) remarkable.

EXAMPLES OF CORE MESSAGES

When first learning how to develop a core message or unique perspective, my clients often like examples. Take a look at Table 1 on the following page; it presents several core messages. Notice how the core message differs from the topic and content. Notice also that each presentation profile—Expert, Interpreter, and Catalyst—must find a core message. No one gets off the hook!

TIPS FOR FINDING YOUR CORE MESSAGE

When developing your core message, you might find yourself lost in the swirl of words and all the possible iterations of them. Here are some tips to find your way out of the confusion.

Say your core message out loud. The act of saying your sentence out loud to another person can help you clarify it for yourself. You will immediately hear which words and phrases you stumble over—things you can't catch when saying your sentence in your head.

Ask someone what they think your talk is about. State your one-sentence core message to someone. Then ask them, "Based on that core message, what would you expect my presentation to be about? What does that one sentence mean to you?" Their response will show you if

AUDIENCE	TOPIC	CONTENT	PROFILE	CORE MESSAGE
Bankers striving for a healthier lifestyle	Nutrition & weight loss	Information about how food affects your weight	Expert	What you eat affects your bottom line.
Individual investors	Bonds	How bonds fit in an investment portfolio	Expert	Bonds are the nerds of your portfolio.
IT & QA teams	Testing process	New process for testing software earlier	Interpreter	Drive quality rather than chase it.
Prospective CIO clients	IT vendor's sales pitch	Large-scale implementation & transformation	Interpreter	Large-scale implementation is what we do best.
Sales & marketing teams	Working together to achieve sales goals	What has worked; ways to extend momentum	Interpreter	We're stronger together.
Supporters of organ & tissue donation	Importance of organ & tissue donation	How each donation benefits many	Catalyst	We enhance lives.
Franchise owners' meeting	Delivering distinctive customer experiences	Anticipation of customer needs	Catalyst	A uniquely satisfying customer experience.

Table 1: Sample Core Messages

your message leads the audience to the content you're planning. If so, nice work! If not, be sure to determine whether it's the *sentence* or your *content* that needs to change.

You could also try the reverse: give your draft talk and ask your listeners what they heard as the core message. Again, if something needs to change, determine whether it's the core message or the content.

Don't get hung up on your one sentence. This piece of advice might sound like I'm contradicting myself, but I'm going to say it anyway: Don't get hung up on your core message. If you swirl and swirl and swirl trying to find the perfect sentence, you risk never moving on to the rest of your talk. Or you find yourself so rushed during the rest of the process that you run out of time for rehearsal.

Get your core message directionally correct, then keep moving. Developing a presentation is an iterative process. You can and will refine your core message as the entire presentation is refined.

HOW TO KNOW YOU'VE FOUND YOUR CORE MESSAGE

Not sure if you've found your core message? Here are the three signs to look for:

1. It describes the essence of the entire talk;

2. It's simple enough to be repeatable; and

3. All your content maps back to it.

As you develop the rest of your presentation, anything that doesn't map back to your core message is irrelevant. Cut it. Your core message is home base.

Not only is it *strategically* worth investing time and energy developing a core message, but *tactically* you'll find it easier to organize, develop, and deliver your presentation as your core message becomes clear.

CHAPTER 11

Organize Your Content

Organize for understanding.

Vikram directs digital marketing for a pharmaceutical company. We spent several sessions preparing a presentation he would give to senior sales leadership.

When initially asked about the context and his intent, he responded: "I need to 1) communicate the power of digital marketing to influence medical practitioners, 2) present high-level digital performance metrics, and 3) engage the sales team to partner with marketing to optimize sales efforts in digital."

Right off the bat, as a listener, I'm overwhelmed and don't know where to focus.

Then I asked Vikram to deliver his draft speech for me.

To get the listeners' attention, he opened with a success story about retention. Then he had an activity to get the audience talking about how much the sales people used digital. Then he showed how medical practitioners used digital.

Then he talked about how the marketing team used digital. But because he had all the different sales and marketing efforts mixed up on his slide, he got the whole audience (me) confused. And then he wanted to start sharing the *real* information: "I do A, B, C, D. This is how it helps you do E, F, G, H. And my job is to make sure that everything gets executed this way."

All of that in five confusing slides. And he just...kept... tripping...up.

"OK," I said. "Let's start with your core message." No surprise—he realized he didn't have one. He had many things to say, but no single message to hang everything on. As we continued to talk, Vikram realized his core message was "We're stronger together," meaning the sales team and marketing team get better sales results when they work together rather than in silos. And that's what he needed them to do—work together.

With that core message we were able to develop an organizational framework that would help him achieve the results he was looking for. Vikram's original speech had two openings, which can easily confuse an audience. We eliminated the success story, and he started by asking the audience, "In the last hour, how many of you have used your tablet or phone?" That gave him a sense of the room and (of course) included almost everyone.

Then he said, "You know what? Our medical practitioners use digital technology just as often as you do. Since the marketing team knows how they use it, we understand how they work. Now we need to combine your sales contacts with the digital efforts we have in marketing—because together we get stronger results."

He went on to show what sales and marketing had done so far. "Working together last year, we reached thousands of practitioners we never would have reached if we hadn't combined forces. Let's keep that momentum going. Here's how we do it…"

We shifted his framework to: the current situation, the impact of the current situation, and how we build on the current situation. Because we're stronger together.

The first time he said this restructured presentation out loud, he finished and said, "Oh my gosh, it flows."

Yes!

The Power of Clear Organization

Time and again I've found that when a speaker trips up in delivery, it's because the content is not structured properly. And when the speaker can't deliver information smoothly, how can the audience be expected to understand it?

If you want your audience to learn something, do something, or imagine something, don't make them figure out what that something is. Make your content crystal clear so they can take it in, add their own experience to it, and move forward. If they have to decipher the key points, they'll be on to something else. They don't have the time or mental energy to do your organizational work for you.

By giving your presentation a clear structure, you give your listeners a map to follow. The content makes sense because the audience can track your talk easily. You don't force them to *figure out* what you're saying. You allow them to *leverage* what you're saying.

Let's look first at organizational principles and how to structure the body of your talk. Then we'll add the open, close, and transitions and put it all together.

Organizational Principles

Two overarching principles about organizational structure guide the rest of this chapter...

Principle 1: Your content must support your core message. Since you've read the previous chapter (Clarify Your Core Message), it won't surprise you to learn Principle 1: Your presentation content must support your core message. Remember, your core message is the one sentence that clearly summarizes the essence of your presentation. Your core message, or unique perspective, is home base. Everything in your presentation must map back to home base. If it doesn't, it's irrelevant. Cut it.

If you really think something needs to be in your presentation but it doesn't relate to your core message, you may need to revise your core message. Creating a presentation is an iterative process; it's OK to make changes.

Principle 2: Your audience can handle two to five main points. Most audiences can handle two to five main points. Anything less than two, and the topic isn't sufficient. Anything more than five, listeners start to tune out.

I once attended a seminar with a well-known marketing guru. He started his talk, "Today I'm going to share thirty-seven different marketing tools with you." My imme-

diate internal response: *Oh my goodness, I'm exhausted already.*
By the time he got to number five, I wanted to raise my
hand and say, "My brain is full. May I please be excused
now?" My guess is the speaker wanted to impress us with
the number thirty-seven: "Look how much I'm giving you!
This is SUCH valuable information!" All it did was cause
me to think, *You're making me work too hard.*

What if our marketing presenter had instead said, "I
have five marketing strategies for you; if you use one tactic
from each, you will leapfrog the competition next year." My
brain would have immediately started counting those five
strategies and actively listening for the tactic I wanted to
use from each.

Do you have more than five main points? It's time to
revisit your core message. What does your audience *absolutely* need to know? Remember, creating a presentation is
an iterative process.

Structuring the Body of Your Speech

Keeping those two principles in mind, let's look at how to
structure the body of your presentation:

1. Gather available information;

2. Group the information into a logical
   framework; and

3. Position your need-to-know information
   within the framework.

STEP 1: GATHER AVAILABLE INFORMATION

In this step, you gather relevant information. Look for specific facts, examples, meaningful statistics, analogies, metaphors, quotes from experts (including your opposition or competitors), and your own experiences.

When you first begin organizing, it helps to lay out all your information on the table (so to speak). Viewing the information you *could* discuss grounds you in your topic and can trigger ideas or identify gaps. There are any number of methods for viewing information: traditional outlining, visuals such as mind-maps or fishbone diagrams, or sticky notes or index cards where each note or card contains one idea. Whatever method you choose, identify what you know about your topic; get it out of your head and make it visible.

As you sort through your information, begin to focus on what your audience truly needs to know. Nice-to-know information, such as irrelevant background material or too much detail, only detracts from your message and leaves your listeners confused and overwhelmed. Remember: Don't make them think! *Providing only need-to-know information is an important differentiator for powerhouse presentations.*

Tip: Use PowerPoint to organize. While I'm a firm believer that you should clarify and organize your message *before* building your slides, I believe that PowerPoint (or similar slideware) can also be a useful tool in these initial steps. Think of each slide just as you would an index card or sticky note—simply in a digital format. Use the slide sorter view to sort your ideas as you proceed through the rest of the process; cut and paste slides the same way you would shuffle index cards or rearrange sticky notes. To be clear, this use of PowerPoint is to assess and organize your content. While it might provide ideas on how to share your content visually, the result is *not* your presentation slide deck.

STEP 2: GROUP YOUR INFORMATION INTO A LOGICAL FRAMEWORK

After identifying all the possible information and culling out some of the nice-to-know information, fatigue often sets in. Many people stop, thinking the brain dump is the talk. While it would be nice to think you're done, this is when the analysis really begins. Now you have to ask questions like: "What is this data saying? What's the story here? What things logically group together? How will it naturally make sense?"

Keeping these questions in mind, segment your content into logical groupings. Categorizing your information benefits your audience because:

- Small pieces of information are more easily digestible than large blocks of complex information, and

- Having related information together creates more meaning, making the information more memorable.

Sometimes grouping your content makes it obvious which organizational framework is appropriate; it emerges naturally, such as grouping similar marketing tools. Other times you'll need to design a unique schematic, perhaps something specific to your business or industry. Your framework becomes the roadmap that lets your audience know where you're taking them—directly and unmistakably from Point A to Point B.

Table 2 below offers common effective frameworks.

FRAMEWORK	EXAMPLE
Past, present, future	Last year our results were this...; this year we are doing this...; next year we envision getting to a higher level by doing this....
Problem, consequence, solution	Our project ran into this problem; as a result we missed deadlines; our solution is to make this adjustment to get back on track.
Theory & practice	Here's what we thought was going to happen when we started the job. Here's what happened in reality.
Who, what, when, where, why & how	To test a new product idea (why), our team (who) piloted an app (what) for our biggest customer (who) last year (when); we collaborated (how) onsite (where) to ensure their needs were met; given our success, the new product is a go.
Bottom line up front (BLUF)	Executive summary: We recommend proceeding with this product because the ROI is huge. Now we'll describe how we made that determination.

Table 2: Sample Presentation Frameworks

There is not one correct organizational structure for any given speech. The right framework for you depends on your unique perspective and how you want to tell your story. Multiple ways could be "right." But the way you'll know you've hit on *a* right structure for a given speech is how it *feels*. Something clicks into place, and the framework makes sense. You don't trip up when speaking; your words flow. Rather than fighting the structure, the structure carries you as you convey the information.

STEP 3: POSITION YOUR NEED-TO-KNOW INFORMATION WITHIN THE FRAMEWORK

Once you've identified an appropriate framework, you can position your need-to-know information within it. (This step may entail more culling of unneeded information.) I envision a wire scaffolding with hooks on it. From each hook hangs a set of information—a story, a set of data, a problem-solution combo, and so on. A colleague likes to think of all his information as a big pile of sports equipment. His segmenting is the equivalent of putting the equipment in piles by sport. Then each sport has its equipment neatly hung on the equipment rack (the framework).

Structuring Your Open, Close, and Transitions

Once you've got your structural framework and you've filled it in with your content, it's time to add the pieces that make it feel complete: the open, the close, and transitions.

OPENING: THE ICEBREAKER

When people first sit down for a presentation, they're not quite ready to listen. Chances are they just came from another meeting, another breakout session, or some other activity. They need a little time to get their bearings. If there's a parade of speakers, your audience needs a moment to bring closure to what they just heard, take a mental break, and then gear up to start listening again.

With this in mind, the goal of your opening is to get your listeners' attention and invite them into the conversation. This type of opening is called an icebreaker. You might also hear it called a "grabber" or "opener."

This is one of those situations in which it's helpful to delineate what *not* to do. Then we'll look at stronger opening options.

HOW NOT TO OPEN

Get out your scorecard. How many of these openers have you heard or used yourself? We've probably all used them at one point or another.

Clichés, platitudes, and thank-yous. Picture a speaker being introduced. She walks to front of the room, shakes hands with the emcee, turns and faces the audience, and the first words she utters are, "Thank you, John, for that gracious introduction." Sigh. Here we go again...

Frequently, business leaders open their presentation saying, "Thank you for inviting me," "It is a pleasure to speak to you today," or "I appreciate your being here" and then quickly proceed to what they really want to say. These are salutations, *not* the start of a talk, and the truth is, the audience merely tolerates them. This default opener makes your presentation feel like it's the same ol' same ol'. While a thank-you won't send the audience running, it does nothing to jump-start a powerhouse presentation.

Tip: If you do feel a need to thank the emcee, offer sincere thanks—eye to eye—when you shake hands. Then dive into your opening remarks with a strong voice, commanding presence, and relevant words.

Unrelated stories or jokes. Have you ever been to a presentation where the speaker opens with a joke or a story and then says, "Well, that has nothing to do with what we're going to talk about today, so let's just dive in." What?! You just took me (your audience) on a pipedream for a minute, and now you want me to instantly come back? No!

Whatever you do in your icebreaker, it *must* lead to your presentation content. Whether you start with a joke, a story, a quote, or a startling statistic, your intent is to invite people *into your topic*. Your first words pave the way, so set yourself up for success.

"Today I'm going to talk about…" "Today I'm going to talk about thirty-seven marketing tactics." "Today I'm going to talk about digital marketing." "Today I'm going to talk about the power of speech openers." More default openers…

Audiences want—and deserve—a much stronger opening, one that grabs their attention and sets the expectation that you are a speaker worth listening to.

HOW TO OPEN STRONG

Avoid the defaults and misfires described above. Instead choose one of the icebreakers described below to arouse your listeners' interest and introduce your topic.

Anecdote or personal story. We never outgrow the magic of "let me tell you a story." Human beings love anecdotes and stories; we're wired for them. And when you tell your own story and share your own observations, that self-disclosure creates a bond with your audience. (Keep it appropriate though—don't disclose so much that you feel vulnerable or your audience feels unsure how to react.)

Example: This book opened with my personal story about Mrs. Griffith's tenth-grade public speaking class. That's exactly the type of story I could use to open a speech about the importance of connecting with yourself, your message, and your audience.

Analogy. An analogy is a comparison based on similarities between two otherwise unrelated items. A well-developed analogy allows the audience to grasp a new, often complex concept by relating it to something familiar. The simpler and clearer the analogy, the better.

Example: "Writing a book is like building a house. First you frame it in (develop an outline or structure), then you put up the drywall (write the first draft), and then you paint the walls (revise). Those tasks need to be done before you bring in the furniture and decorations (edit and proofread). Imagine spending hours picking out the perfect pillows for the sofa; then you realize the sofa is too big for the living room and has to go back! That's why you revise before you proofread."

Question. Asking your audience a question—sincere or rhetorical—is an excellent way to open a presentation. A well-chosen, relevant question can involve the audience and get them thinking about how the message applies to them and their situation.

Example: "What did you have for breakfast? Really—
think about what you had for breakfast. How did it affect
your day?" [Pause.] "Did you know that what you eat—or
don't eat—for breakfast affects your mood and metabolism
for the rest of the day?"

Quotation. Sharing a relevant quote can instantly unite and focus your audience. The quote doesn't have
to be from an icon like Jeff Bezos or Oprah Winfrey. The
source can be a colleague, something you read, or a client's
endorsement of your company.

Example: "Confidence is life's enabler. It is the quality
that turns thoughts into action." —Katty Kay and Claire
Shipman, *The Confidence Code*

Current event. Using a current event to introduce
your message can capture your listeners' attention, especially if it's highly relevant to your topic. Do keep in mind
that if a current event took place too many news cycles ago,
it can make your presentation feel dated. If you're comfortable making last-minute changes, read the morning news
and add something extremely fresh.

Example: "Yesterday's unexpected stock market drop is
one of the most compelling reasons to have a portion of
your portfolio in bonds. Stocks might be flashy, but 'nerds'
create stability."

Startling statement. Share a simple, striking statement or a little-known fact that is relevant to the core message of your presentation. The more unusual or surprising,
the better. This approach can trigger a range of audience
emotions that make them want to know more.

Example: "There are 115,000 people on the organ
transplant waiting list in the U.S. That's like filling up every
seat in MetLife Stadium—PLUS another 32,500 people."

Do you see how much more effective these icebreakers can be than the stock "Thank you. Today I'm going to talk about..."? Whichever opener you choose, it's only effective if it is both attention-getting and relevant to your topic.

You can make your icebreaker even more potent by circling back to it in the close.

CLOSING WITH POWER

Many speakers blurt out "Thank you" when they're done with their presentation, because they hope those words will clue the audience in that it's over. But "thank you" at the end is nearly as weak as "thank you" at the beginning. Nix the thank-you and make your concluding statement the exclamation point that lets people know you are done.

First, give the audience an indicator you're coming to a close. You don't necessarily have to use phrases like "For my final point..." or "In conclusion...," which can seem too "default," but do alert them that you are about to conclude by restating your core message and summarizing your main points. They will be grateful for the opportunity to catch anything they may have missed during your speech.

Then, make your ending resound—give your audience a "haymaker." In boxing, a haymaker is a forceful blow or knockout punch; in speaking, it's the closing statement that drives home your message with impact. Since it's the last thing you say, you want it to be important, be memorable, and offer a sense of coming full circle.

One way to bring resonance and reinforce your message is to refer back to your icebreaker. This is sometimes called "bookending" your speech.

For example:

- Story – If you start your presentation with a story, end with the story's conclusion.

- Question – If you began your speech with a question, offer the answer at the end. Or ask a variation of the question to reinforce insights the audience gained during the speech.

- Startling statistic – If you started with a statistic about a problem, offer a follow-up statistic that shows, for example, what happens when your solution is used.

Your haymaker gives you the opportunity for one final memorable statement, so grab the chance to end strong!

Tip: If you structure the body of your speech first, it becomes easier to design your icebreaker and haymaker effectively.

TRANSITIONING BETWEEN POINTS

Transitions are simple phrases or brief sentences that help people see how one thought leads to the next. While transitions are presented last here, that doesn't mean they're unimportant. On the contrary, transitions are critically important, and yet they're one of the best-kept secrets in public speaking. If you can use transitions well, your audience will have no trouble following your train of thought. *This is a differentiator for delivering a powerhouse presentation!*

A transition gives your listeners a signpost that orients them to what has been discussed already and where they're headed next.

There are several ways to do this, including:

- Summarize – "Before I go on, let me summarize the points made so far…"

- Review/preview – "Now that we understand the importance of customer service, let's look at steps to improving service in our stores."

- Enumerate – "The first issue we covered was… The second issue is…"

See how simple it is? Unfortunately, many people rely on their clicker to indicate a transition. They talk about one slide, finish, and click to the next slide, assuming the audience knows they've changed topic. Click, click, click with no connector. Most business leaders do this without even realizing it.

Remember, your goal is to get your message across as easily as possible so you can achieve your endgame. If you don't have a transition, you force your audience through the mental gyrations of keeping up ("Wait, *what* topic are we on now?"). Instead of forcing them to connect the dots themselves, take them to each succeeding point clearly and smoothly. Let them save their brainpower for the real message and what it means to them.

Putting It All Together

You have all the components of your speech; now it's time to put them together.

Your **introduction** captures the audience's attention. It comprises about 10% of the presentation and includes:

- An icebreaker to grab the attention of the audience, and

- A preview to introduce your core message, or unique perspective, and to reveal the main points detailed in the presentation body.

The **body** of your talk explains and supports your core message. It comprises 80% of the presentation and includes:

- A reiteration of your unique perspective, and

- Your 2–5 main points with credible supporting material (and transitions between points).

Your **conclusion** summarizes the entire presentation. It comprises 10% of the total presentation and includes:

- A review to summarize the main points, and

- A haymaker to provide a resounding close (and give listeners a sense of completion).

Clarifying your message and organizing your content go hand in hand. I've said it before and I'll say it again: creating a presentation is an iterative process. Don't be afraid to keep refining your unique perspective and adjusting your framework. When speakers make their presentation delivery look easy-breezy, it's usually because they've spent time getting their messaging right.

CHAPTER 12

Develop Your Audiovisuals

Help your audience learn more in less time.

John, the vice president of a utility company, called me in to help him with an upcoming speech. He delivered his draft presentation for me—along with *sixty* PowerPoint slides.

We reduced the number of slides to twenty-five.

He gave the presentation again.

We reduced the number of slides to twelve.

He gave the presentation again.

I said, "John, you could do this without any slides. The slides are actually tripping you up—and they're not adding value to your message."

He was not quite sold on this idea, but he tried it again without slides.

Later, on the way to his meeting, he called from the airport. "I want you to guarantee me that if I don't use these slides, these people are still going to take action."

"John, I can't guarantee that, but what I can tell you is they'll hear your message a heck of a lot better."

And they did. He delivered his message confidently—without slides—and got the action he needed.

The Purpose of Audiovisual Support

Why do I start a chapter on audiovisual aids with a story about *not* using them? It goes to their purpose: audiovisual (AV) aids are there to *aid* the transmittal of your message. If they don't aid, don't use them.

However, when used appropriately, visual aids have an undeniable impact on audience retention. There's no easier way to improve audience comprehension than with the right use of visual support. Dr. Robert Haakenson (a.k.a. "the Haak"), my first post-college mentor, used to say, "AV aids help you say more in less time."

There are three main reasons to use AV support: to explain concepts, to keep your listeners oriented, and to re-inforce your message.

Explanation. When you are explaining a concept, a visual aid can sometimes clarify in seconds what would take minutes to describe. For example, if you're describing a conference space to the speakers, show them a photo of the room—it instantly gives them a better sense of the environment. The conceptual becomes real.

Orientation. Visual aids can also help direct your audience or keep their attention focused. For example, if you're describing a process, you could use slides to keep your listeners oriented as you proceed through the steps.

And when you are describing data, even if it's not complex, a visual keeps the audience grounded.

Reinforcement. Visuals can drive home your message in a way that words alone cannot. When I present about teamwork, I use an image of my son and me tethered together rock climbing to emphasize the need to support each other. When I teach the C.O.D.E. process and we've finished Clarify, Organize, and Develop, I always say, "Now that you've made it through that, Express will be a piece of cake," and I show an image of a nice big gooey piece of chocolate cake. How can you use AV to punctuate your message?

Remember the dictum "Don't make me think." Your AV support should help your audience take in your message as easily as possible, so they can take the action you need.

Types of AV Other than Slides

Because PowerPoint is such a corporate standard, this chapter focuses on the effective use of slideware. You might use Prezi or Keynote or another tool, but the same principles apply. Before we jump into that, remember there are other audiovisual options available that you may overlook if you default to slides.

WHITE BOARD OR FLIP CHART

White boards and flip charts are great for smaller presentations or working sessions in a conference room. Consider drawing relevant diagrams in real-time or capturing audience ideas and feedback on the fly. These two options might be a little trickier on a large conference stage, but they're not impossible. At a recent conference, a flip chart was critical to a main-stage presentation. To make the pages visible to the audience, the video crew angled one camera at the flip chart and projected it to the screen where PowerPoint slides would normally appear. Be creative!

OBJECTS

It's easy to forget you can pick up an object to show people something. Even on a big stage with several hundred people in the audience, it can work.

In his Raleigh TEDx Talk "5 ½ Mentors That Will Change Your Life," Doug Stewart shared the story of being told he was stupid at age eleven.[4] He held up the sheaf of papers where his teacher had written a description of how he struggled for fifteen minutes to write the alphabet—and still didn't get it right. The couple hundred people in the room didn't need to read the comments; seeing the papers was enough. They immediately understood how this assessment would influence his self-image for the next several years, until a college advisor helped him reshape his thinking about ADD and dyslexia.

If you're making a presentation on athletic shoes with the latest innovations in technology and design, consider bringing a few sample pairs to pass around. If you're talking about stress relief and work-life balance, throw koosh balls into the

4   Doug Stewart, "5 ½ Mentors That Will Change Your Life," June 7, 2016, TEDxRaleigh, 17:46, https://youtu.be/quhcyPpCaSk.

audience. If you're asking your convenience store employees to maintain a neat, clean environment, show them a dirty apron as an example of what customers *don't* want to see.

Objects can be powerful support for your message.

VIDEO

Video is the growing medium in today's business world—anything from short clips made on a phone to expensive custom productions.

At a large IT firm that provides enterprise-wide solutions to Fortune 500 companies, it's common for executives at the highest levels to get involved in the sales process. In fact, when the CEO cannot make a high-stakes meeting in person, he records a custom message for the prospective client. The sales team plays the video as part of the pitch, an effective use of video.

Peyton Holland is the director of SkillsUSA North Carolina and a regular speaker about the next-generation workforce. In his keynote "Skills That Pay the Bills...and Redefine Success" about vocational education,[5] Peyton first shows a large bowl his father made from black walnut. He goes on to play a video of the machine his father used to make the bowl: a homemade contraption pieced together from an old lawnmower motor, scrap metal, and a few pulleys. It's a genius use of an object and a video together to make his point. Nothing else—short of having the machine on stage—could capture it as effectively.

5 Peyton Holland, "Skills That Pay the Bills...and Redefine Success," June 9, 2016, TEDxRaleigh, 16:52, https://youtu.be/6OvVlkx69Ys.

If video helps you make your point, use it; but think twice if it's just for flash. Your AV needs to support your message and your endgame.

AUDIO

A somewhat less common but still effective form of media is audio. Yes, you hear walk-in music at big events, but that's not what I mean. Rather, how can you use audio to support your message?

For example, imagine you're talking about customer service and the top priority projects for the coming year. You could play the audio of what the automated phone system sounds like when customers call in—and how frustrating it is for them. If web accessibility is your topic, play a recording of what it sounds like when a visually impaired person uses a screen reader—show how unintentionally poor design choices make it more difficult to understand.

Or how about this one... A pharmaceutical company had a new product to help children with attention-deficit/hyperactivity disorder (ADHD) cope with sensory overload. At the product launch, the lead-in to the presentation was imagery of children at play, accompanied by an audio recording of sounds appropriate to the image—laughter, shouting, and so on. As the images progressed, the audio was layered so each sound continued as new sounds were added. It built to a cacophony that was almost deafening and then it...STOPPED. There was silence (to everyone's relief) as a single black slide with white type appeared: "ADHD." Everyone in the audience "experienced" the condition, which created a breakthrough moment for them to remember the impact the product would have for children affected by ADHD.

Powerful.

PEOPLE

Have you ever thought of a person as an audiovisual aid? Stan Phelps, author of *Purple Goldfish*, regularly tells a story of being on a business trip in New York. While waiting for a colleague to join him at a bar (and sipping a $14 beer), he strikes up a conversation with a stranger and takes away some important lessons about expectations. Stan has written up the dialog from that conversation on notecards, and when possible he invites someone from the audience to come up and play the role of the stranger. The audience gets to watch the whole conversation play out, rather than having just Stan relate it. Clever.

PowerPoint and Other Slideware

When PowerPoint appeared in the business world, people became fascinated with it, especially with animation. They began to spend more time on fly-ins, builds, and other slide animations than on what they had to say and why they were saying it. "PowerPoint" became synonymous with "presentation." The length of a talk began to be measured by the number of slides, and Death by PowerPoint arrived.

I resisted PowerPoint for the longest time, but finally accepted it had become a standard in the business world The challenge was to help my clients use it *effectively*.

WHAT IS THE PURPOSE OF A SLIDE DECK?

When PowerPoint is your focus, it's easy to forget the real purpose of your presentation: to connect with your audience in order to achieve your end goal. As with other AV support, **the purpose of the slide deck is to support your message by aiding audience understanding**. Slides should capture the essence of what you're saying and provide the audience insight, allowing you to communicate more in less time.

Too often a slide deck becomes a de facto teleprompter or an all-inclusive list of everything the speaker knows about the subject. That approach results in text-heavy slides that Garr Reynolds, in his book *Presentation Zen*, calls "slideuments." When you project a slideument onto a screen, your audience becomes so busy reading that they don't listen to anything you say. If your content can be distributed and clearly understood without you (the presenter), you've created a document, not a deck that supports your presentation.

There is one good use for a slideument: when you are not speaking to an audience, but rather sharing a large amount of data or findings in a work session. You can distribute your detailed deck to be read in advance, which gives your audience a chance to digest all the information, and then use the meeting to summarize and position the data for discussion or decision-making. But recognize this is really a document, not a slide deck. The document is the focus, and you are simply the voiceover talent there to provide verbal navigation.

SIGNS YOU'RE RELYING TOO HEAVILY ON SLIDES

Not sure if you're using PowerPoint appropriately? Check for these signs of relying too heavily on a slide deck:

- You can't give the presentation without the slide deck.

- Your presentation consists only of reading aloud what's on your slides.

- You look only at the computer screen to read the slides, and forget to look at your listeners to connect and see their responses.

Why do people keep plodding down the typical, tedious PowerPoint path? "That's the way I've always done it!" "They're only giving me fifteen minutes and I've got a lot to say." "People will need all this information when they get back to their offices." (Be honest, how often do you go back to a PowerPoint for reference? Others probably don't either.)

As I mentioned earlier, PowerPoint *can* be a useful tool to help you think through your presentation—what to say and how to say it. But getting your thoughts down is just the first step. Can you imagine sending a rough draft of your quarterly report to your board of directors, thinking it's done?

Now it's time to step back and ask those same questions you've asked before:

- What does your audience really need to know?

- How do you talk about it in a way that makes sense to *them?*

Remember your core message and organizational framework, and use a Glance & Grab strategy to quickly ground your audience so they can turn attention to you.

GLANCE & GRAB STRATEGY

Driving down the road, you check your rearview mirror. How long do you look? A second? Less? In an instant, you're probably doing several things, from seeing if you're being tailgated to making sure you won't get a speeding ticket. Those brief moments involve important, even critical, decisions.

Now apply that same thinking to your PowerPoint. Imagine you have only seconds to help your audience get what you're talking about. What information will they need? What's the best way to communicate it? Should you use words? Pictures? A combination of the two?

Whatever you choose, make sure your listeners can **glance** at your media and **grab** what they need, so their attention returns to you as the speaker. Don't use anything that takes the attention away from you and your message.

- If you have to say, "I know this is too small, so let me tell you what it says," it's not Glance & Grab.

- If you have to use a laser pointer to show people which part of the slide to look at, it's not Glance & Grab.

- If you have to say, "I know there's a lot on this slide," it's not Glance & Grab.

Your listeners have a million other things going on in their heads. If you take up their mental energy by forcing them to figure out your slides, they're off to bigger and better things.

Here's the exception that proves the rule...

I was working with a software engineer who had a very complicated slide. I said, "Mamma mia, that slide is so complicated!" He replied, "Thank you. That's exactly what I want you to say when you look at it. My whole point is to show the audience how complicated the current process is. If I clean up the slide, they won't get it."

He knew exactly what his core message was: "This process must be simplified." And he knew that words alone would not suffice. To get the message across to his audience, he needed a correspondingly messy visual. He intentionally wanted the *opposite* of Glance & Grab! Now imagine following up that complicated slide with a new process that was clean and easily understood. Yes.

RSVP PRINCIPLES

To implement the Glance & Grab strategy, apply the RSVP principles: Relevant, Subordinate, Visible, and Pictorial.

RELEVANT

When you use any kind of AV support—PowerPoint especially, but also video, flip charts, and other aids—it must be **relevant** to what you're saying, doing, or asking in that moment. The goal is not to give the audience something to decipher or to distract them; it is to maximize the impact of your message.

To ensure your visuals are relevant, review them with a critical eye. Ask:

- Is each slide pertinent to what I'm saying at that moment?

- Is the media adding value, or is it just a filler?

- Am I using slides as a crutch to remember my talking points? (Ask this especially about slides with bullet points.)

Cut out everything that does not support what you're saying when you say it. If it makes you nervous to pare down your slide content, move the detailed information into the speaker notes, so you'll still be able to reference it. As a bonus, if you write the notes to be understandable to others, you can use those printouts as your audience leave-behind, eliminating the need for a separate document.

Watch out for bullet points. A slide full of bullets is always a red flag. Most people use too many words in each bullet (sometimes multiple lines' worth!). As a result, the bullets become visually distracting, because the audience spends too much time figuring out which one the speaker is on.

If you must use bullets, make sure each one is relevant. Keep phrases short and pithy; use the fewest words possible to help people get what they need. And, if possible, reveal bullet points one at a time using a "build" so the audience stays oriented without being distracted.

Use visual cues. An IT consulting firm had a matrix of data and wanted to talk to their client about one particular number in it. When they put up the entire matrix, their audience started picking apart the numbers. The entire conversation got wrapped up in one number—a number completely irrelevant to the intended discussion!

Two problems: First, the IT company put *all* the data on the slide. Did all the data need to be there? Probably not. Second, assuming all the data *did* need to be there, it was displayed without any sense of priority or focus. Each number was the same size and color; there was nothing that visually differentiated the relevant number, so of course it was easy for the clients to get distracted by the first thing that caught their attention. How would this conversation have gone differently if there had been a big red circle around the relevant number?

Use color, shading, and other visual items to direct the audience's attention. Put a shaded box behind the section that illustrates what you're talking about. (See Figure 2.)

Use callout boxes, arrows, or big red circles to focus attention on the details you want the audience to look at. Even better, change the color in the rest of the visual to make it appear grayed out. (See Figure 3.)

What to do when you don't have a slide. There may be stretches of your presentation with no visual. That's OK! But don't leave the prior slide up; it's irrelevant once you move to your next point. Instead, use an interstitial slide, which is a slide that displays neutral information, such as your presentation title or an image of you (the speaker). Or, make the screen black or white by pressing your keyboard's B key for black or W key for white; when you're ready to bring up the next slide, press B or W again. Tip: Some clickers also have a button for black-screen functionality built into them.

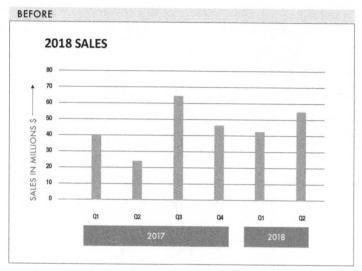

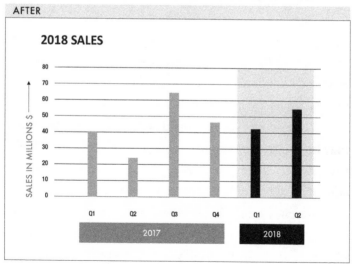

Figure 2: Using Shading and Contrast to Highlight

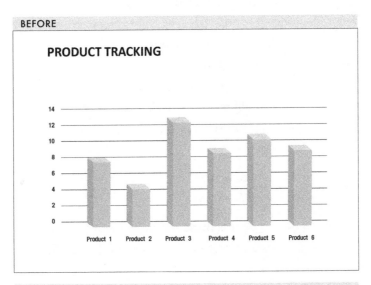

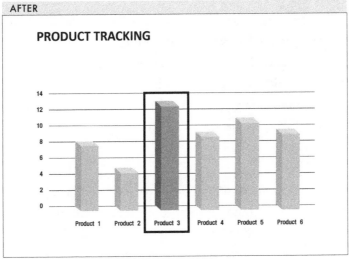

Figure 3: Using Box and Contrast to Highlight

SUBORDINATE

You are the headline act. Don't be upstaged! In our IT example above, because the client got distracted with one number, the slide became more important than the speaker and the issue being highlighted.

Instead, make sure your slides support you. Listeners should be able to glance at the visual and grab the essence of your message, and then quickly return their full attention to you. Ask:

- Is the media subordinate to me? Am I the headline rather than a subtitle?

- Could I give this presentation without the supporting visuals? (If not, it's time to rethink your approach.)

When your audience walks out of your talk commenting on how gorgeous your slides were, yet can't remember your message, the slides have taken precedence over you. Slides that do an exceptional job of conveying the message leave people saying, "I got it. Great information!" or "I understand what we need to do—let's go do it!"

VISIBLE

Every slide you use should be visible (and audible if there is sound) to the standing-room-only crowd leaning against the back wall—in the amount of time allotted. To this end, you will hear any number of rules about PowerPoint. The 10/20/30 rule, the 5/5/5 rule, the one-slide-per-minute rule, and on and on.

Instead ask yourself: "How do I help my audience learn more with less?" If you can show the audience three slides in sixty seconds and they have enough time to comprehend them, great. As presentation guru Nancy Duarte advises in the *HBR Guide to Persuasive Presentations*, "Don't worry about slide count. Just make your slides count."

Consider:

- Are the fonts large enough that your audience can read all the text from the back of the room?

- Can your audience comprehend the content in the amount of time allotted for each slide?

- Is the sound audible to everyone in the room?

One strong guideline: aim for a font size of 30 points minimum. At that size, unless you are in a *very* large auditorium or conference hall, your entire audience should be able to read the text. A bonus of using 30-point font (or bigger) is that it limits the space available on the slide, requiring you to think about what's really needed and what can go. You are forced to edit. Do note that two different fonts might be the same point size and yet appear different due to their style. When in doubt, go back to the questions above.

PICTORIAL

Finally, your slides should be pictorial; that is, they should use visual imagery. The combination of visual and oral presentation improves information retention. Additionally, when you're not tied to specific words on the slide, you're free to focus on the audience, and the audience is free to focus on the message. In turn, the message can be more easily heard, and listeners are more inspired to act. However, you should not use pictures for pictures' sake. They need to be relevant to the content, such as an illustration that helps explain what you're saying or an image that punctuates your message.

For example, at the National Association of Convenience Stores, the board chair rotates each year. Part of the executive team's preparation with the incoming chair involves telling their personal stories. They've got wonderful photos to go with the stories: board members as children sitting under the cash register at their parents' store, the first store they owned, what their store looks like today. "Oh, Bailey, weren't you cute!" "Oh my goodness, look at you doing homework under the register." The images make the executives relatable on a human level.

Another example: NJ Sharing Network's staff and volunteers work tirelessly on communications about organ and tissue donation. This is hard work. I wanted to see if we could make their work a little easier by helping their listeners connect with the message emotionally.

Overall, the PowerPoint slides they used were text- and bullet-heavy, which held the speaker captive to the words on the slides. After learning the RSVP approach (especially Pictorial), they gave their slides a makeover, replacing text with captivating images. The example in Figure 4 is typical of what changed.

Reflecting on the change, Jackie, manager of foundation development, commented, "The impact was immediate and remarkable. We're presenting the same information, but in a way that's much more inspiring. Rather than being passive listeners, our audience members hear our message and participate in the conversation; they want to help."

BEFORE

Who is NJ Sharing Network?

- Organ Procurement Organization (OPO)
- Private, Non-profit Service Organization
- Federally Designated
- State Licensed
- Available 24 hours/7 days a week
- Arrange for the recovery of all organs and tissues for transplantation

AFTER

Figure 4: Revision from Bulleted to Pictorial Slide

CHAPTER 13

Express Yourself & Engage Your Audience

*There are enough ways in the world
for everyone to have their own.*

Richard owns a chain of convenience stores. Several years back, he was preparing to speak at the annual National Association of Convenience Stores (NACS) show. At the time, NACS was battling on Capitol Hill to address credit and debit card "swipe fees," which cost the industry around $10 billion each year. In his main-stage presentation, Richard was asking NACS members to stand up and take action—to write their congressperson. It would be difficult to get people to do something as unsexy as writing a letter to a lawmaker, so he needed a way to fire up the crowd.

While Richard was talking, he had a ticker behind him showing how much money swipe fees were costing the industry every second the audience sat in the room. He developed an impassioned talk about the issue and planned to wrap up with an echo of the famous speech by the character Howard Beale in the movie *Network*: "So I have a question for you. Are you mad as hell? And are you not going to take this anymore? Then write your representative."

But it was just too tame. I said, "Richard, you can't stop there. You've got to get the audience up and have them yell it back to you." He was reluctant to do something so over the top, but, with enough prodding, he did it.

Here is the segment from his talk (formatted as it appeared on his teleprompter):

Do you remember

the movie Network*? Academy Award winner in 1976?*

Do you remember

the main character, Howard Beale,

and what he says?

If you don't, I'm sure you will recognize

the line he made famous:

"I'm as mad as hell,

and I'm not going to take this anymore!"

So, I want to know...

Are you mad?

Are you mad as hell? If so,

stand up and yell,

"I'm as mad as hell

and I'm not going to take this anymore!"

Thousands of people stood up and yelled, "I'm as mad as hell, and I'm not going to take this anymore!"

It took a couple more years, but retailers ultimately prevailed on the issue.

Expressing Your Best Self

Imagine if Richard had ended with a calm call to action without getting the audience on its feet. How many people would have been inspired (or even remembered) to take action?

Your posture, movement, gestures, facial expressions, eye contact, and voice all can enhance or impede your message. Working with clients on their delivery, I try to help them do three things: align their words and delivery, allow their natural talents to shine, and eliminate distractors.

CREATE ALIGNMENT

I recently saw a speaker conclude his presentation by saying, "I welcome any discussion about the information I've shared. Does anyone have a question?" He said this while gazing down at the floor. Because he said one thing ("Question?") while his downward gaze said something completely different ("Please don't ask me any questions!"), no one raised a hand and the presentation came to an awkward, abrupt close. No doubt you've witnessed something similar.

One of the most important aspects of expression is alignment between your message and your delivery of it.

Contradictions in a speaker's words and body language or voice jeopardize their credibility. The best presenters get everything working together—their words, body language, facial expression, and voice, as well as slides, props, or other audiovisual support. When all aspects of your presentation are in sync, you'll find that your audience not only gets the message, they'll be inspired to act.

USE YOUR NATURAL TALENTS

Actors portray characters on stage; however, when you're a business leader, you need to be the same person off stage as on; people know when you're not. That's why it's important to be 100% present as your very best you. No facades allowed. Audiences want to see amazing, authentic, individual speakers.

You have natural talents and abilities you bring to the table. To talk on water, you have to let those assets come to the surface. One of the first things I do with clients is watch them deliver their presentation. How do they present themselves? What are their strengths?

Natural talents can be simple things like a great smile, strong gestures, or good posture, or less definable traits such as being approachable or being a good storyteller. Everyone has something that shows up as a natural talent—something built into their DNA. *That's* what I try to highlight, because those are the things that make the biggest contribution to connecting with their audience.

Not sure what your natural talents are? That's OK; strengths feel so normal to us that we often don't recognize they're special. Just ask someone; get feedback from colleagues about where you shine when you present. And when they answer, *listen.* Don't dismiss what they say. When someone tells you what you're good at, don't give them ten reasons you're not. Take in the feedback and allow yourself to acknowledge your natural talents. You may be surprised!

Having an understanding of your strengths lets you build on them and amplify them so you're confident and credible and speak with conviction.

ELIMINATE DISTRACTORS

If you've ever been involved in process management efforts such as Six Sigma, you may be familiar with the concept of a control chart, a tracking tool that monitors key performance metrics. As long as performance stays within the desired boundaries, things run smoothly. As soon as something goes out of bounds, the control chart throws up a flag indicating, "Hey, something is getting in the way of a smoothly running process!"

Apply the same concept to your presentation: What's getting in the way of smooth communications between you and your audience? Is something causing a disconnect? Are you doing anything that makes it more difficult for your listeners to receive your message? Maybe you use verbal fillers (ums or ahs), wander aimlessly, or adjust your glasses repeatedly. All of those things are distractors. Eliminate them.

For instance, I recently coached several clients who were prepping for the same event. One woman was extremely likeable (natural talent), but she eroded that strength when she cocked her head and talked with an upswing at the end of her sentences (distractor). Once I brought these two items to her attention, she could focus on aligning her head with her posture and modulating her voice. However, these mannerisms also often indicate discomfort with content; since the uptalk continued, we edited her content as well.

Another woman in the group was charismatic. She had fantastic posture, great eye contact, and excellent content (natural talents), but she spoke so quickly (distractor) that her audience couldn't connect with her message. To maintain her strengths but mitigate the distractor, she decided to ask rhetorical questions periodically. The questions allowed her to pause for breath while the audience caught up.

Your job is to speak in a way that your audience can hear your message and take it in. When you align your words and your actions, build on your natural talents, and eliminate distractors, your mission is accomplished. While this chapter only scratches the surface of platform skills, the goal is for you to understand the principles involved so you can find your own style.

What Language Does Your Body Speak?

Even seasoned presenters can be uncomfortable getting up in front of an audience. When you feel this way, your body language often reflects your emotions. You may unconsciously stand in a closed posture, limit your movement, or use weak gestures—making you appear less confident.

Growing up, when I faced something that made me nervous, my Auntie Terry would give me a pep talk. "Stephanie, stand tall, shoulders back. Hold your head high, take a breath, and smile. Remember, you are a SCOTTI!" Today, those words still echo in my head when I'm about to walk to the front of a room to present.

THE SPEAKER STANCE

The speaker stance is all about using your posture to communicate presence and poise. Auntie Terry's advice was sound. Stand tall and erect with your shoulders back. Your feet should be shoulder width apart, with your weight evenly distributed. Imagine your legs are trees with their roots going right down into the floor: you are grounded.

If it's more comfortable for you, place one foot slightly in front of the other. This position helps avoid a tendency to rock and prepares you for movement. (But look out for the two-step—one step forward, one step back, one step forward, one step back; don't make your audience seasick.)

Relax your arms at your side. Keep your elbows slightly bent with your hands at about waist height. This position primes you to gesture. And, frankly, if you stand like this very long, you'll feel silly, so you're *forced* to gesture.

While the speaker stance may feel awkward until you've practiced it a while, it helps you project a confident and professional presence. Your posture and stance are foundational to the physical delivery of your presentation.

INTENTIONAL MOVEMENT

Moving with intention demonstrates confidence in yourself and your message, emphasizes and reinforces your message, and creates inclusion and connection with the audience.

Walk onto the stage with a stride that communicates your pleasure to be there. As you make your way to the front, imagine filling the room with your energy to build the crowd's anticipation of your presentation.

Throughout your speech, use movement that supports what you're saying. If you want your listeners to pay attention to a slide or consider what you're saying, *stop moving*. If you want to emphasize the past, present, and future, start on the right of the stage for the past, move to the middle for the present, and move to the left for the future. *Stop in each location*. Avoid "dancing," pacing, and aimless wandering; they only distract the audience.

Most important, move across the stage or around the room to include all members of your audience. On a large stage, come closer to the front of the stage if possible. Imagine three "bus stops"—one far right, one middle, one far left; walk to each and stop there for a portion of your speech. In a conference room, if you must stay in one location, pivot your body to face each section of the audience directly. Everyone wants to be included.

GESTURES: NUMEROUS, PURPOSEFUL, AND VARIED

Being Italian, I need gestures to talk. You need them too, even if you're not Italian, because gestures help people understand your message. You already use your hands in casual conversation; let that movement become a natural part of your enlarged conversation with the audience as well. Make your gestures numerous, purposeful, and varied.

Look for words, phrases, or concepts in your presentation that naturally invite expressiveness. Mark your notes with suggestions—not so you deliver a scripted performance, but as a reminder as you rehearse. Consider universal gestures such as "stop" with your arm extended, or "give" and "receive" with motions indicating that action. Find opportunities for emphasis (for example, punching your hand in your fist) or places for description where you can indicate size or speed. Consider how you would indicate "from one end of the spectrum to the other" or "we've been looking down here in the weeds and now need to take a 30,000-foot perspective."

Gestures help get your message across. Bonus: By using the bent-elbow speaker stance described earlier, you stand ready to gesture with muscular control.

MATCH YOUR PHYSICAL PRESENCE TO THE ROOM

Your stance, movement, and gestures are essential to projecting a confident, professional presence. The magnitude of your physical presence can make the difference between appearing like milk toast (limp and wimpy) or like Texas Toast (big and bold).

In a smaller speaking situation, such as a meeting in a conference room, your natural gestures come from your lower arms—elbow to wrist. This style is appropriate and works well in a setting where you're physically close to the audience. Moderate motions serve to emphasize your points without being too overpowering.

However, the same gestures and stances you use with a small group come across very differently in a large setting. When addressing a big crowd from a stage, these small, lower-arm gestures make you look like you're shrinking.

To command the presence needed to gain your listeners' attention in a large space, use the speaker stance described earlier. But this time, stand with your arms slightly extended in front of you, with palms up as though you're handing something to the audience. As you speak, use your shoulders to lift your arms higher and gesture with your entire arm as if you are reaching up and out to your audience. Your whole body opens up, and you appear larger.

This may feel huge or even over the top to you, but will look normal to the audience. You get their attention and show them your desire to connect, which in turn makes them want to listen to what you have to say.

The larger the space and the greater the number of people, the bigger your gestures and stance must be. Additionally, the larger the space, the slower you need to move. Just a slight decrease in speed helps your audience members better follow your gestures and movement, and connects them with what you're saying.

The Talking Head

Have you ever noticed how often presidential candidates are criticized for how they look? The severity of their "neutral" expressions, their lack of *any* expression, their poor eye contact with the audience or with the camera (you can't win for trying sometimes). We constantly judge others and make decisions about them based on how they look.

Luckily, giving a business presentation doesn't earn you quite as much scrutiny as being a political candidate, but you need to be aware of what your face is communicating.

FACIAL EXPRESSION

When you speak, your facial expression helps your listeners interpret your words. A monotone face requires your audience to listen *harder*. Instead, strive for animation, and match your facial expression to your words. Happy words, happy face; serious words, serious face. It's that simple (of course using the full spectrum of emotions). Beyond that I offer two pieces of advice…

Smile. Smiling makes people instantly feel comfortable and welcomed. A genuine smile lights up your eyes even before your lips move, telling your audience you're sincere. When someone smiles back at you, you know you've engaged them. Even if you don't outright smile, maintain a pleasant neutral expression. Try lifting the muscles at your temple—it perks up your eyes and delivers an almost-but-not-quite smile. Practice this one while waiting in line at the store, driving your car, or sitting at your desk.

Watch out for the head tilt. When you listen to a question or try to understand someone, it's common and natural to tilt your head. However, if cocking your head becomes a default position, it gives the audience the impression you're asking, "Did I get it right?" or "Do you like me?" That is *not* the impression you want to give in a high-stakes business presentation. Straighten up so you appear both attentive and confident.

EYE CONTACT: DIRECT, ROVING, AND CONTINUOUS

Participants in the U.S. Army Corps of Engineers' Leadership Development Program (LDP) had to deliver a 45-minute briefing to the brigadier general and senior leadership team as their final exam. I was there to help them prepare.

They impressed me right from the start. Each of the twenty-three participants greeted me with a strong hand-shake while looking me straight in the eye. Holding my gaze for just those few moments communicated confidence, credibility, and connection. These are big words for such a simple gesture, and yet direct eye contact conveys that, and more. It says, "I am important—and so are you."

As a presenter, using your eyes to engage your audience is critical to creating a sense of confidence, establishing credibility, and building rapport. The overarching guideline: during your presentation, **maintain a minimum of 90% direct, continuous, and roving eye contact.** *Strong eye contact is a differentiator for powerhouse presentations.*

Start with direct eye contact. After you're introduced, but before you say a word, stop, look out at your audience directly, and smile. This "power pause" allows your audience to get settled, helps make a strong connection, and establishes your authority. It may feel awkward at first, but it's not that different from how you greet a houseguest when they enter your home—fostering a sense of hospitality that allows people to connect with you. Your power pause establishes your presence as a leader. I repeat: *this strong eye contact is a differentiator for powerhouse presentations.*

Speak to the eyes. When speaking to a crowd, you may be tempted to use a soft focus on the whole group or several people at a time. You may want to give your attention to your notes, slides, flip chart, or the back wall. Or you may—without even realizing it—speak *past* your listeners.

Instead, look directly at individuals within the crowd and speak to their eyes. Hold eye contact with a person for about three seconds, and then move to the next. Or, look at one person until you've finished making a point, and then move to another person for your next point. The principle is to appear comfortable making eye contact without darting around the room suspiciously or drilling holes in people. If it helps, find a few people who are smiling, nodding, and showing support and focus on them.

When you look out at your audience, be continuous and roving. Look at *everyone*—from the front to the back, from side to side, in the far back, in the middle, and even in the balcony if appropriate. (Tip: Focus on a head in the distance rather than trying to make direct eye contact with someone far away.) Notice if you tend to favor one side of the room, usually the side of your dominant hand; you may find it helpful to visually divide the room into sections so you address all of them. Turn your head, pan your body, walk around the stage, or even walk out into your audience to make sure you include everyone.

End with direct eye contact. When your presentation is complete, you might want to beat a quick retreat. If you do, you'll be doing yourself and your listeners a disservice. End your remarks by looking out, scanning the audience, and smiling. Like putting a period at the end of a sentence, this gesture signals completion. It allows your listeners to know you are done and, if appropriate, thank you with a round of applause. It also gives you a chance to breathe and connect with your audience one last time.

The Four Ps of Vocal Expression

When coaching for vocal expression, I begin by encouraging clients to use a conversational tone. Just talk with me like we're having a relaxed conversation over a beverage. Once that conversational feeling is there, we can look at how to punch things up to come across effectively on a larger stage (figurative or literal).

Let's look at the basics of the four Ps: power, pace, pitch, and pause.

POWER

Power refers to volume: how loudly or softly you speak. First and foremost, you need to be clearly heard and understood everywhere in the room. If you're not using a microphone and are concerned you may not be heard, ask your listeners to raise a hand if they're having difficulty hearing you. They'll be happy to help—and may even pay closer attention to what you're saying.

Your vocal power also conveys emotion. Using more vocal power gives you energy, authority, and conviction; you naturally speak in a louder voice when you want to get listeners fired up. Conversely, a soft voice can draw an audience in to your more subtle, intimate points. Don't be afraid to go soft, as long as you can still be heard.

PACE

Pace is how quickly or slowly you speak. Many people speak too fast because they're nervous (or unprepared), making it difficult for the audience to follow. At the opposite extreme, speaking too slowly or at an unvaried rate has put many an audience to sleep.

Make a conscious effort to vary your vocal pace. Slow down for important or complex information so that listeners can process and understand. Speed up to highlight familiar points and keep listeners engaged. If you struggle to slow down, practice pausing in places you would use a comma in written language; just take a breath. Sometimes you can get away with a fairly rapid rate as long as you let your listeners catch up periodically.

In a large space, just as your movement and gestures need to be a tiny bit slower, your pace needs to be a tiny bit slower to help your audience keep up with your words.

PITCH

Pitch refers to the rise and fall of your voice as you speak. When your pitch is too extreme (high or low) or too monotone (lacking inflection), it can be unpleasant to listen to and cause your listeners' attention to wander. A natural, conversational tone provides vocal variety and indicates your passion and excitement about the topic.

My client Sasha had the problem known as "upspeak," or "uptalk"—that tendency to end each sentence with a raised pitch so it sounds like a question. Like a head tilt, this habit is fine in small doses, but when overdone it implies a lack of confidence that can damage your credibility. While historically this problem has occurred more with women, it's been cropping up recently among younger men as well. Instead, use a downward inflection pattern that gradually returns to your ideal conversational pitch as you reach the end of a sentence.

PAUSE

Pause refers to the space between sentences, phrases, or words. Think of pauses as verbal punctuation marks. They help your audience understand and relate to your words by providing micro-breaks to process information and to rest. Pauses also give you time to breathe, and breath gives you more power and control of your pace.

Many speakers are uncomfortable with silence, so they fill the needed space with "um," "ah," "like," and "you know." We're all human, so a few filler words here and there aren't usually a problem in a business presentation. However, if a pattern develops—if people start tallying up how many times you say "so," "um," or "like," turning it into a game—you've got a problem. When your audience is distracted by filler words, they're not focused on your message. Not only do you sound less credible and less professional, but if you don't breathe, your voice lacks energy and isn't compelling. If you use too many fillers, train yourself to pause instead, because after all, fillers are pauses in your thought pattern.

Another troublesome pattern that has appeared in recent years is a pattern of talking in short phrases. "Hello, my name is. Stephanie Scotti and I. Teach presentation skills." As much as I love TED Talks, this pattern seems to show up frequently in them. Sometimes it works; in business, it often does not. Any sort of predictable rhythmic punctuation like this quickly becomes a distractor. If you too are a TED fan, make sure you're not picking up this habit from watching videos.

Real pauses at the right frequency punctuate your message, add weight and gravity to what you say, and give your listeners the necessary time to digest what's being said.

A NOTE ON ACCENTS

I've worked with people from all around the world: Russia, Turkey, China, Spain, the United States, India, Ireland, Germany. When they express concern about their accent, I always tell them (and truly believe) that their accent is part of their charm—it's part of what makes them unique.

If you have an extremely heavy accent and people regularly have trouble understanding you, you may want to pursue some help with accent modification. But for most people, the trick is simply to slow down and pause, so the listeners' ears can catch up, adjust to the accent, and process the information. An accent is not a liability; it's part of your appeal.

Three Delivery Myths

During rehearsal for a large conference, I noticed the staging for the keynote speaker included a small round table. When he came on, he placed a green file folder on it. Throughout the presentation, he played a series of short videos. While the videos had the attention of the audience, he took the opportunity to walk over to the table and, much to my surprise, he reviewed his notes. No one else in the audience knew his secret, and I suspect that his occasional review of his notes allowed him to customize his remarks on the fly.

Brilliant. This was an experienced speaker who knew not to believe the first of three common delivery myths.

MYTH #1: YOU CAN'T USE NOTES

People often believe that being an effective presenter means speaking without any type of script or notes. Not true, as evidenced by our keynoter above. If having your script, outline, or notes close at hand makes you more confident, that confidence will help forge a strong bond with your listeners. The trick is to refer to your hard copy while staying connected—maintaining eye contact 90% of the time. How?

- Don't be married to the exact words on the page.

- Be clear about the *intent* of your presentation.

- Number your pages so if they get out of order, you can quickly and easily find your place. (I learned this one the hard way.)

- Be comfortable enough to continue to gesture, even with your notes in hand.

Most important, practice out loud so you know what you want to say. That way, you can simply glance at your notes and grab what you need to continue your thought. (Glance & Grab—sound familiar?)

MYTH #2: YOU MUST STAY BEHIND THE LECTERN

A lectern is a stand that holds your notes and often a microphone. (A podium is the platform the lectern, and you, may stand on.) Many speakers mistakenly believe that if there's a lectern, they must stay behind it. To the contrary, all other things being equal, you will better engage your audience if you periodically leave the lectern or leave it completely and move freely about the room or stage. However, it's OK if you do prefer to stay at the lectern (say, to be near your notes), and sometimes you don't really have a choice due to the limitations of the setting.

When you present from a lectern, you have an object between you and the audience, which means you must work extra hard to connect with them. In addition to good eye contact and animated facial expressions, stand tall. A strong, erect posture always projects a confident and professional presence, but it's especially important with an object in front of you. Additionally, avoid the lectern death grip; white knuckles only tell the audience you're uncomfortable. Instead, focus on gestures—and make sure to get them *above* the lectern so the audience can see them.

While there may be a physical barrier, there needn't be an emotional one.

MYTH #3: IT DOESN'T MATTER WHAT YOU DO IF THE AUDIENCE CAN'T SEE YOU

At some point, you've probably delivered a presentation where listeners were not able to see you. This happens with webinars, podcasts, quarterly analyst calls—all those events with audio but no video or only fixed slides for images. Sometimes even at live events where the audience *can* see you, such as an analyst summit, people are so busy taking notes or looking at their devices as they follow along that they don't look at you.

When you know your audience won't be looking at you, it's tempting to let up on your delivery skills. This is a missed opportunity, because everything you do (or don't do) to engage your body comes through in your voice. When your body lacks animation, your voice comes out flat and dull. If you sound bored with your own message, why should your audience pay attention?

Beyond engaging your audience and achieving the results you're after, your delivery impacts your own sense of accomplishment. Use the skills described in this chapter, and walk away from every presentation knowing that you did your best to ensure your audience understood your message and is able to take action.

Engage: Q&A Discussion

In a speakers' networking group, the discussion was about where and how people got tripped up in their presentations. Q&A—the infamous question and answer session—came up as a natural tripping hazard. While some people loved Q&A, others said they got nervous, afraid they'd be caught off guard and unable to answer a question.

Ray, spontaneously and with quite some vigor, blurted out, "I hate Q&A! I don't like it when my audience asks me questions. Who are they to question me?" The group laughed. He was so defensive there was no point in trying to offer a different perspective.

Ray clearly viewed Q&A as a confrontation. I'd rather view it as a conversation. It is an opportunity to invite dialog. But I do understand the anxiety that can come with not knowing precisely what to expect. So, let's take a look at how to manage your Q&A session effectively.

PREPPING Q&A

Part of your presentation preparation should indeed include careful consideration of the range of questions you may receive. You've already done audience research; that's one source for identifying potential questions. You can also brainstorm with your staff based on their experience or anecdotal information. You can even ask audience members what questions they have as they arrive at the event. These conversations prepare you to listen openly as well as craft appropriate responses. Just as rehearsal calms your nerves about giving your speech, preparing for questions helps eliminate worries about being tripped up.

TEEING UP Q&A

To tee up Q&A with your audience, promote it before and during your presentation. If an agenda is distributed, make sure it mentions the Q&A discussion so participants can give thought to their questions in advance. As you begin your talk, you or the person introducing you can say something like, "There will be fifteen minutes at the end of the presentation for your questions, and comments are welcome as well. Please jot down any thoughts you have so we can talk about them." *Asking for both questions and comments will boost participation and is a differentiator for powerhouse presentations.*

STARTING Q&A

The transition between your speech and your Q&A should be smooth, as if it is simply a continuation of a conversation. After concluding your remarks, pause briefly and acknowledge any applause before introducing the Q&A. Say something along the lines of "Now we have ten minutes to hear what you have to say. First question or comment please." Look expectantly at your audience and be prepared to wait a few moments for that first hand to go up.

When you invite participation and wait for the Q&A to start, it is critical to maintain eye contact with a smile or pleasant facial expression. If you drop your eyes for even a moment, your audience may interpret it to mean you don't really want anyone to participate. Try silently counting to ten while looking around the room; that's usually enough time for people to gather their thoughts and work up the courage to speak.

What if no one has a question? Sometimes you just need to give it a few more seconds; eventually the nervous energy in the room will increase enough for someone to raise a hand. If not, you need to determine if there's really no interest or if people just need a nudge to get started. After a long day of breakout sessions, or before lunch, your audience may be tired or hungry and ready to disengage. If you open Q&A to minimal response and people packing

their bags, take their cue. Proceed to your final statement.
But more often, they just need encouragement.

Here a few ways to jumpstart participation:

- Have a plant in the audience. If you suspect
you'll have a shy audience on your hands, arrange for someone in the audience to start off
the Q&A with a question or comment prepared in advance.

- Based on your past experience or research
about your audience, bring up a common question that you believe will be of interest to them.

- Take a poll. Ask the audience members to express their opinions or share experiences about
an issue you addressed in your presentation.

FACILITATING Q&A

Now that your Q&A is off to a good start, build on the
momentum of that first question or comment. Continue
to look expectantly at your audience: "Next question or
comment, please." Then answer and facilitate using the
following techniques.

Recognize people by name or location. Instead
of merely pointing to someone whose hand is raised, say
something like, "Celia, what's your question or comment?"
or "Let's hear from the gentleman up front with the green
tie." This simple gesture easily identifies individuals and
keeps things moving. In some situations, there may be a
microphone positioned in the center aisle; even then, if you
recognize the person stepping up to speak, feel free to use
their name or ask them to introduce themselves.

Set up a batting order. During your Q&A, set up a "batting order." Just like a baseball game with the line of players waiting their turn to come up to the plate, queue up your listeners to ask questions. This technique is especially helpful if your topic is emotionally charged or if the audience has considerable energy around the topic. A batting order helps you take control of the dynamics in the room.

Say something like, "Let's start with the gentleman in the fifth row, then let's come up front and hear Mary's question or comment, and then over to the far right—the man leaning against the wall." Now you've established a rhythm; everyone knows what to expect and people don't have to sit there with their hands in the air. What's more, using a batting order helps prevent you from spending too much time on one question by providing an easy way to shift the focus and move on. Once you've answered the first question, simply say, "Let's move on to Mary."

Do a listening check. If you don't understand a question or comment, or if you are concerned that audience members may not fully understand, ask for clarification using a listening check. In your own words, repeat back what you understood the question to be, and ask the listener to verify that you got it right. If not, allow them to further explain. This simple step prevents misunderstandings and helps you respond smartly.

Keep responses short and sweet. Listeners don't want a long, drawn-out discourse for each question. Answer as succinctly as possible; try to keep your response to no more than forty-five seconds. Keeping responses concise allows you to answer as many questions as you can in the time allotted.

Avoid asking, "Did I answer your question?"
When you finish answering, avoid tag-ons such as "Did I answer your question?" Particularly in a heated discussion, this opening can fuel the fire and keep you trapped in a one-on-one conversation. Trust that you answered; move on so you keep the rhythm going and maintain control of the room. Listeners can always raise their hand again if they have additional questions to ask or comments to make.

Handle a potential embarrassment with grace. If the listener has forgotten her question, simply say, "We'll come back to you in a moment." If the listener indicates that his question was answered, smile and say, "Great, if there's something else you'd like to ask about or comment on, please let me know. Let's hear from Graeme in the third row…" Minimize a potential embarrassment for the audience member, and certainly never belittle anyone.

Remember you don't have to be omniscient. If you don't know the answer to someone's question, say so. If possible, it's a nice gesture to offer to get the answer within a reasonable period of time. Simply ask the listener to jot down the question on her business card and hand it to you after your presentation concludes. Doing this allows you to serve your listener without the distraction of asking for contact information. But don't feel you have to track people down to collect their question; if it is important, they'll find you and let you know how to get in touch with them.

ENDING Q&A

How often have you attended a presentation that ended with "Well, we're out of time, so thank you very much for coming"? We're so accustomed to this that we accept it as normal, but wrapping up your presentation this way is a missed opportunity to end strong and make your message memorable. It's much more effective to plan for and close your Q&A in a way that shows respect for your audience and allows you to end strong. *Ending Q&A properly is a differentiator for powerhouse presentations.*

Manage time to manage Q&A expectations. To end properly, manage time effectively throughout the session, so your audience can manage their expectations. When you kick off Q&A, tell your audience how much time you have to respond to questions and comments. Then, when you're about 75% of the way through, let people know how much time is remaining. Say something like, "We have about three minutes left; time for one or two more questions."

Doing this helps your audience anticipate what's coming and respond accordingly. If you say you have time for one more question and there are still ten hands in the air, a listener will realize that you won't be able to get to her question. She can then decide to write it down and email it to you later. You establish a level of trust when you tell your listeners what you're going to do and then follow through.

Quit while you're ahead. Even if you're not under a time constraint, don't keep the Q&A going too long. The purpose of Q&A is to have a brief, shared interaction with your listeners, not to give another presentation. It's much better to end with questions unanswered than to milk the audience dry. Anticipate the wind up. As either time or interest seems to be running out, announce, "We have time for one more question or comment. Whose will it be?"

End smartly on your own words. If you conclude your presentation with a quick thank-you following the final question or comment, you're actually ending on someone else's thought. Instead, be prepared with a final closing sentence or two—no more than about thirty seconds' worth—that reiterates your core message. If you are good on the fly, consider wrapping up with a theme that emerged during the Q&A, still incorporating your core message. This final statement ties everything up and closes out your presentation and Q&A together.

Once your session concludes, stick around. Many times, an informal Q&A will develop after the formal presentation has ended.

Done well, Q&A engages your audience in a highly effective and rewarding way. The more questions asked, the more listeners are engaged in what you have to say. And the more dialog there is, the greater understanding you have of what your listeners will do with the content you shared. To achieve your endgame, that's exactly what you want.

PART FOUR

Preparing for Prime Time

CHAPTER 14

Prepare & Rehearse

Preparation, not desperation.

Angelo was preparing for his first keynote presentation at an annual association meeting. I asked him what the environment would be like. When he told me how many people would be there, along with other staging details, I said, "You need to prepare for the lights."

He insisted there weren't going to be enough people there to have special lighting.

I suggested he call the conference planner or executive producer and ask for additional details about the setting.

"No, no, no."

I offered to give him a list of specific questions.

"OK, OK, OK, I'll call."

He never did.

You can guess what happened: the stage was lit and he couldn't see a thing. It threw him so much he couldn't speak for what felt to him like a full minute.

Carving out time to prepare for logistics and rehearse a presentation may seem like a luxury. But to achieve the results you need in high-stakes business presentations, preparation is an absolute necessity. It's the silver bullet that eliminates desperation and increases confidence.

Would you take an exam for a professional certification without studying? Would you give a piano recital without practicing? Would you run a marathon without training? Have you ever heard anyone say they regret having pre-pared? *Thorough preparation, including rehearsal, is a differentiator for powerhouse presentations.*

Basic Logistics

Even as you begin working on your presentation, it helps to have a feel for the logistics of the event: venue and space; staging, room setup, and lighting; and equipment and AV support. You can't always control the logistics, but being familiar with them helps you avoid surprises and prepare effectively. It may even influence how you craft your talk. Having a higher comfort level with the logistics (whether for a ballroom or the conference room down the hall) allows you to be flexible and responsive to whatever happens.

Pre-Show Practice

If you've reviewed your presentation in your head and feel prepared to deliver it to an audience, think again.

Until you've rehearsed out loud multiple times, you can't truly tell what works and what doesn't, what trips you up, what's too complicated, or what just doesn't sound like you.

Rehearsing also gives you a solid idea how long your talk takes. I've been to major events where the stage would go dark or strobe lights would start if presenters exceeded their time. *You do not want that to happen to you.* And even if the overtime rules aren't so severe, your audience does not want you to go over time. Ever. And if there is another speaker after you, for sure *they* don't want you running over.

Rule of thumb: a presentation that's "done" on paper is probably about 70% done in reality. On average, it takes **five focused practice sessions** for a business leader to really seal the deal, especially when it comes to critical or career-defining presentations. Certainly, preparing for a weekly staff meeting report doesn't demand five rehearsals. But when the pressure's on, there's no replacement for a structured rehearsal plan to help deliver results.

Here's what rehearsals look like...

READ-THROUGHS AND EDITING

When putting on a play or making a film, one of the first things the cast does is sit together at a table and read their parts aloud from the script. This read-through, or "table read," is an opportunity to identify problematic areas in the script and to get the actors familiar with their roles and how they interact. It's also a signal the preproduction phase is complete and it's time to move into production mode.

Your first two or three rehearsals are table reads. You've developed your presentation, and you have a script or notes; now you need to shake out the bugs. Read your presentation aloud to assess its flow and length. Fine-tune your message so it feels and sounds like you. Each time you work through it, continue tightening your message and confirming your timing. Flow and timing; flow and timing. You can do the first couple rehearsals on your own, or you may bring in a trusted colleague to offer feedback and help with revisions.

Keep in mind, rehearsal doesn't always need to be formal. You can practice saying your speech out loud while driving to work; if you like to sing in the shower, try giving your speech in the shower. The point is to develop confidence about what you're saying and how you're saying it.

PRACTICE FOR DELIVERY

Around the third or fourth practice, as your words get ingrained in you, begin to focus on delivery skills. Make sure any props (including your slide deck) truly support the content. Ensure all your points get the intended weight and significance. If you'll have a teleprompter or confidence monitor, begin practicing with it; if you feel uncomfortable with it, you still have time for Plan B.

During these rehearsals it can be helpful to have a friendly, small practice audience. Emphasize to them that you are open to what they have to say; encourage them to candidly share their comments and ideas. Tips:

- Ask for specifics – Rather than "You need more gestures," ask for "Using gestures when you say

X would really emphasize your point; here's a type of gesture that might work."

- Clarify, don't debate – Ask questions to clarify any comments that are unclear, and graciously accept all feedback. You are not obligated to adopt every suggestion, and you can always get a second opinion.

- Use the fifteen-minute test – Ask your listeners, "If I only have fifteen minutes to make changes, what would you suggest I do differently?" With this approach, you can distinguish the must-do's from the nice-to's.

PREPARE TO ADJUST FOR TIME

As you rehearse, recognize that things don't always go as planned the day of the big event; you may have to adjust your presentation to a shorter or longer time frame. Being prepared for that will ease any anxiety you might feel.

Adjusting to a longer time frame is not usually too much of a problem. Most of us have relevant content we can include (not filler!), or the Q&A session can be extended so the audience has input into the additional content.

Adjusting to a shorter time frame can be challenging. There are two basic approaches you can take:

- Cover all your main points in less depth, or

- Cover fewer main points.

Say your presentation has five main points with supporting material that you can cover comfortably in a thirty-

minute time frame. If you are given only twenty minutes
because the prior speaker ran over, you may decide to cover
all five points with less detail in the supporting material. Or,
you may decide to narrow your focus to only four of the
five main points so you can maintain most of the detail in
the supporting material. Choose what is most useful to your
audience.

However, if you are given only ten minutes for your
thirty-minute presentation, it may be difficult to cover all
five main points in any meaningful way. In this case, you
may be better off narrowing your focus to the top two main
points. How do you determine which those are? Go back to
your audience analysis and core message: What does your
audience *absolutely* need to know within the time allotted?
You must be discerning.

Nancy Duarte, author of the *HBR Guide to Persuasive
Presentations*, always develops two endings, each at a natural
stopping point. If there's plenty of time, she uses the later
ending; if time is tight, she can stop at the earlier one—and
the audience is none the wiser.

Regardless of which strategy you choose, there is one
thing you should *not* do: talk super-fast so you can squeeze in all your
content! And remember: it's almost always OK to finish early,
but it's never OK to run over.

On-Site

Many presenters stop short and don't rehearse at the actual
venue. Take advantage of an on-site rehearsal to orient
yourself to your surroundings and make sure your equip-

ment is set to go. This will both bolster your confidence and allow you to prepare for any last-minute changes.

TECH REHEARSAL

If you're at a large event where there's a production crew, there's often a scheduled technical run-through (a.k.a. tech rehearsal). The goal is to familiarize you with the staging and equipment and to make sure everything works. Get to know the production team. The sound engineer, teleprompter operator, and stage manager are all your new best friends. Listen to their direction, ask questions if you don't understand something, and let them know if you have a special request.

You won't have unlimited time at a tech rehearsal, so here's where to focus. (Even if you're at a smaller event without a crew, the same basic principles will apply in terms of what you need to pay attention to and prepare for.)

Get oriented. Get to know the room and the staging area so you are comfortable with the space. Confirm the location of confidence monitor or teleprompter. If you'll be sitting, as can occur in a panel, make sure you practice getting in and out of whatever type of seat is provided.

Rehearse your entrance and exit. There is usually a plan for entering and exiting the stage, and you should know what to expect. This seemingly simple step has tripped up many presenters.

Test your media. If you have slides, run through them. Do they display correctly? Who will be clicking—you or someone else? Check any video or audio clips you are using.

Do an audio test. What kind of mic are you using? If a lavalier mic or over-the-ear mic, make sure you know how the battery box clips onto your clothes.

Practice your introduction. Depending on the size of the event and how it is organized, you may be introduced by another speaker or by the "Voice of God" (a.k.a. VOG) over the audio system, or you may find you'll be introducing yourself. Not knowing how you're going to be introduced can lead to a shaky start, especially if the person introducing you says something you don't expect, or if they haven't practiced it themselves.

Practice your open and close. You often won't have time to test your entire presentation at a tech rehearsal. If that's the case, ask the production crew if you can run through your opening icebreaker and closing haymaker.

Wear your shoes. It's common to wear a new pair of shoes to a presentation, but this can be a mistake if the shoes turn out to be uncomfortable. Whether old or new, wear your "presentation" shoes to the rehearsal. (Remember Barbara, who bought new shoes at lunch and got distracted by them?) Women, if you're wearing heels, make sure you're comfortable navigating any stairs or carpets.

PRIME TIME

It's finally the big day. You're well prepared and now you just need to get yourself in the zone.

Perform your pregame ritual. Similar to many professional athletes, experienced speakers often perform a pregame ritual to get themselves into performance mode. You may meditate, do push-ups, sing your favorite song, take a few moments of solitude—whatever helps you connect with yourself and in turn be able to connect with your message and your audience.

Test the equipment. Plan to arrive at your venue, whether it's a conference room, boardroom, or ballroom, at least thirty minutes before you anticipate your audience members' arrival. Make sure everything is working—audio, video, PowerPoint. If something isn't the way you need it to be, you'll have time to get it fixed or implement Plan B.

Transform the room. Get comfortable. Walk around and explore the room. Mentally transform the room from an impersonal space to a welcoming, cozy area, perhaps the favorite room in your house.

Meet & greet your audience. Take the time before your presentation to circulate and get to know your audience. Introduce yourself, shake hands, and ask individuals about their interest in your topic and expectations of your presentation. Informal pre-event conversations can provide spontaneous anecdotes you can use to personalize your presentation and keep everyone engaged. Build rapport before stepping up to speak.

Here's an example of the importance of preparation and rehearsal...

Venky was the CEO of a biopharmaceutical company in search of a manufacturing partner for their product. I worked with Venky to prepare for a "pitch and partner" event. He would have ten minutes total for both his pitch and Q&A from the possible investors and partners in the audience. If he exceeded his ten minutes, strobe lights would go off. (Really. It happened to several of the participants.)

We worked and worked on his presentation, honing his core message and simplifying his slides, but he struggled to narrow his message. Instead of focusing on his core message—his ask—he was trying to be all things to all people.

We scheduled a live rehearsal with a qualified audience—people who understood the investing world. As Venky worked through this rehearsal and responded to thought-provoking questions from the practice panelists, he started to understand the need to focus.

He amped up his revision efforts and got his presentation to six minutes and seven meaningful slides that described the product, the need, and the ask.

The day of the event, he covered all the critical information and finished right at the six-minute mark, which left him *four full minutes for Q&A*—40% of his presentation time and far more than anyone else had.

Rehearsal was a competitive advantage that allowed Venky to differentiate himself and his product. He had investors following him out the door to talk further. Now *that's* a powerhouse presentation.

CHAPTER 15

Manage Fear & Nerves

ARM yourself.

While teaching at Duke University, I worked with a woman who would put her hand on her heart whenever she gave a speech. When asked why, she responded in all seriousness, "Can't you see how hard it's pounding?"

As soon as she made her statement and saw the class's reaction (no, we couldn't see her pounding heart), she laughed.

Then she immediately put her hands over her ears because they turned red—as if cupping her ears were somehow less obvious than a tinge of color.

The things nerves make us do…

This book would be incomplete if it didn't touch on one of the most common adult fears: fear of public speaking. Even those who seem outwardly calm, composed, and confident experience anxiety when stepping too far outside their comfort zone. If you don't learn to address fear and nerves, doubt may creep in and you can have trouble connecting with yourself.

The Truth about Fear

The prevailing wisdom around quelling fears and developing confidence has commonly included strategies such as silencing the critical voices in your head, repeating affirmations until you believe them, and pretending to be confident so you'll feel that way ("Fake it 'til you make it"). You've probably tried some of these suggestions yourself and, like many, found them less effective than you hoped.

Science shows us fear is a survival mechanism hard-wired into the human brain. The fight-or-flight response goes back to prehistoric times when our ancestors needed a shot of adrenaline to overcome the life-threatening situations of their daily lives. This fear is not a weakness, but rather a normal and natural response to risk—and it shows up as negative thoughts, physical reactions, and sometimes both. It's no wonder the tactics above don't work.

The truth is, negative thoughts and physical reactions are not inherently problematic. After all, they're the result of your brain and body trying to anticipate what can go wrong so you can be prepared for it. It's only when you allow these things to prevent you from moving forward that they become destructive. In fact, rather than attempt to eradicate fear, seasoned business leaders learn to live with it—and indeed, use it to their advantage, especially during high-stakes presentations.

ARM Yourself

To address fear, "ARM" yourself: Acknowledge, Reframe, and Manage.

ACKNOWLEDGE YOUR FEELINGS

Fighting hardwired negative thoughts can be like swimming upstream: exhausting and futile. The next time you catch yourself thinking *I'm not sure I'm the right person for this presentation* or feel your heart racing, recognize it's just your prehistoric brain sending you false danger signals.

Rather than fight those negative thoughts and physical reactions, acknowledge them. The simple recognition of fear diminishes its hold and diffuses its power.

REFRAME THE SITUATION

Now reframe the situation. If you're having negative thoughts, shift to: *Hey, there's a reason I was asked to make this presentation!* If you have a physical reaction, take a step back and consider whether your "shortcoming" is real or imaginary—and if real whether you're blowing it out of proportion. Our bodies often fool us.

Deb, a director at a major pharmaceutical company, was a reluctant speaker giving a talk at a high-stakes internal event. When given the option of a handheld mic or lavalier mic (the kind you clip on your lapel), she worried that if she used a lav the audience would be able to hear how fast her heart was beating. By acknowledging her fear to the sound engineer, he was able to reframe the situation for her: of course the mic wouldn't pick up her heartbeat, but she could use a handheld if it felt more comfortable.

While Deb's physical reaction wasn't noticeable, I have one that is: when I get nervous, I blush bright red. I've even had people say, "Do you know you're turning red?" My response? "I know. It's part of my charm!" Much to my chagrin, blushing is something you truly cannot control; it's the real Stephanie showing up. By acknowledging it internally (or when brought to my attention) and reframing it as part of my special appeal, I don't take offense. What else is there to say?

MANAGE YOUR REACTIONS

With clearer perspective, you can begin to choose how to manage your reactions. While you may not be able to completely eliminate unruly reactions (I still blush), you may be able to tame them by working off the nervous energy. I've had some clients do push-ups to burn off adrenaline. Others have gone for a brisk walk. My mentor Dr. Haakenson used to sing "The Star Spangled Banner."

If you still have a physical reaction, what workaround can you find to help mitigate it? If you perspire or feel so hot that you're distracted from focusing on your audience, Matt Abrahams, author of *Speaking Up without Freaking Out*, suggests taking an ice-cold water bottle on stage. Simply hold the bottle periodically as you deliver your presentation. The coolness will soothe and help reduce your core temperature. Plus, a water bottle is a natural thing to carry on stage. (Just don't inadvertently start gesturing with it!)

Need more ideas? Check out Table 3.

ISSUE	HOW TO MANAGE IT
Dry mouth	Gently bite your tongue
Too nervous to advance slides	Have someone do it for you
Talking too fast	Ask someone in the audience to signal you if you need to slow down
Afraid you won't be heard	Ask listeners to give you a thumbs up if you need to raise your voice
Voice quivering	Take time to inhale before you start talking, then speak on the exhale
Catch yourself doing the 2-step	Imagine your legs as trees with roots going into the floor
Shaking	Lightly rest your hand on a table or lectern for a moment

Table 3: Tips to Manage Nervous Reactions

One CEO I've worked with has perfected his personal formula for managing anxiety when speaking at high-stakes events:

- He prepares. Fear often stems from discomfort with content, so this CEO works for clarity and conviction about his message; as a result he builds confidence and reduces anxiety.

- He recognizes his job is to help his audience understand and act on his message. By focusing on his audience, he redirects his energy so he feels self-assured rather than self-conscious.

- He practices, and he involves others in his practice sessions. By soliciting feedback from staff and peers, he gains firsthand knowledge about what works and what doesn't. This helps him build the confidence to handle anything unexpected.

Part of connecting with yourself is understanding what happens to you mentally and physically when you present. Fears and physical reactions might be uncomfortable, but they aren't usually going to hurt you. When you anticipate those things and find workarounds, that alone—knowing you have things under control—boosts your confidence and increases your executive presence. The things that caused anxiety no longer matter.

Fear of Feedback

It's easy to advise people to get feedback as they develop their talk, but for many people the feedback process can be just as nerve-wracking as going on stage. Keep in mind that "feedback" does not equal "negative." Feedback is just data. It's information about your audience's perception of you and whether you're achieving the results you want. If you can get comfortable with the discomfort of hearing feedback, you'll see how it can be a make-or-break tool.

For example, my client Marcey was preparing a keynote presentation. She gives business talks frequently, but this one was different—it was based on a life-altering personal health experience, and she was emotionally tied to the story. She described her initial reluctance to ask for feedback: "I almost felt like it would be easier to just do the presentation and not practice it for anybody ahead of time. The story was so personal that I didn't want to hear any negative feedback." But as a professional, she knew she had to move beyond that fear.

As she began developing her presentation, Marcey asked me and others for individual feedback and found she'd gotten caught in the common trap of information overload. Much of what she'd included was terribly important to her, but much less important to her audience. She continued honing the content down to the need-to-know information. Then, with some trepidation, she scheduled a table read with ten people. Her primary goal was to test the clarity of her core message. She wanted to make sure they received a thought-provoking global message, not a "poor Marcey" message.

The table-read audience told her they understood the gist of her story, but that the speech was still too Marcey-focused without a clear core message—disappointing *but extraordinarily valuable* information. This session provided the "aha" that let Marcey shift her thinking from "telling my story" to "helping my audience get it." Afterward she said, "Getting that feedback was hard—especially in a group, but I suddenly realized I had to separate my personal feelings from the business of my presentation. *This speech was not about my feelings.*"

She continued to hone her message and content, and then tested a version of the speech on stage with a live audience. Again, she received feedback that surprised her and led to additional revision. Marcey continued rehearsing and soliciting feedback as she crafted what can truly be described as a powerhouse presentation—one that has generated unsolicited emails and comments from audience members telling her how resonant her message is.

Just like every other skill we attempt to master, speaking has a learning curve. As you practice taking necessary action in spite of your fear, the discomfort becomes more familiar and feels less risky. By coming to terms with your fears, shifting your perspective, and having a personal plan for success, you'll find that presentations come together with much less anxiety.

"If I can do it, anyone can."

Remember Carla, who was told "You're going to fail" before every speech? To regain a healthy mindset, Carla applied every strategy, tool, and process in this book. Clearly, she'd had her confidence eroded at her prior company and deserved the assurance that the audience did indeed want her to succeed. I promised her there was another way to do things—*her* way—and together we'd explore what that was.

Recognizing this presentation could have a significant impact on her position as the new kid on the block, Carla's personal goal was to establish both authority and approachability as a VP. To help her audience get her message, we made sure her content was well organized and flowed smoothly; it had a strong core message running through it with a clear call to action (Interpreter).

Carla understood and was relieved to learn it was connection, not perfection, that would be her mark of success. She realized nothing terrible would happen if she made a mistake (and most likely the audience wouldn't even know). In terms of her delivery, we focused on authenticity and built on her natural talents. The skills she used so intuitively to connect with her staff were the same skills she would use when speaking...simply bigger and louder.

With practice, feedback, and support, Carla was able to move past years of being told she would fail. "I practiced multiple times with Stephanie and on my own, so the day of the speech I felt prepared. My heart was pounding, but once I started speaking I knew the speech so well it just flowed. Getting through that speech in front of 500 people after six weeks on the job and having people come up to me and say I did great was a huge relief and definitely a positive boost. I still get nervous and my heart still races prior to going in front of a group, but I don't feel that sheer terror I used to. I smile when people say that I'm good at public speaking, and respond, 'If I can do it, anyone can!'"

Was Carla perfect? No, and *that was never the goal.* Carla achieved her endgame: she left the impression she wanted while getting the action she needed. And since then, the line of business Carla runs has doubled in size, approaching $1 billion in annual revenue. Taking nothing for granted, she continues to invest the time and energy to prepare for company-wide strategy meetings.

Preparing for a high-stakes presentation is hard work. Dealing with fear and doubt (and trust me, it exists at every level) takes energy. Turning a same ol' same ol' presentation into a powerhouse presentation requires effort. *But you don't have to do everything at once.*

Focus on one thing at a time. Remind yourself of a foundational belief, determine your presentation profile, clarify your core message, or refine your visuals. If you focus on improving *one thing*, everything else will calibrate and improve as well. When you've gotten comfortable with that one thing, move on to the next thing. Learning is a lifelong process.

I love what I do. I love working with business leaders because I get to learn something every time. I get to learn how they think and why their message is important. I get to connect with them on an interpersonal level. And in the end, I get to watch them connect with their audience, which is such an incredible, powerful moment. I get to see them *achieve.* And when they achieve, they see the benefit of the investment they've made in learning new skills and doing the hard work of preparation—they see the advancement of their cause.

In the opening chapter I shared with you a fundamental lesson my dad taught me at a young age. "Stephanie," he said, "you are unique because of who you are. If you compare yourself to anyone else, you're always going to feel *less,* because there will always be someone better than you. Or you'll get too high on your horse thinking you're better than everyone else and never reach your real potential. *Just be yourself.*"

Thank you, Dad. You taught me that every person is unique. You taught me that there are enough ways for everyone to have their own. You taught me that embracing our gifts and expressing our individuality is what makes anything seem possible—even the ability to talk on water.

ACKNOWLEDGMENTS

Everyone who has touched this book during its creation has added value—actionable feedback that helped me shape the structure, choose stories to include, and hone my concepts and language. I am both humbled and grateful to have so many talented contributors and supporters.

Thank you to my powerhouse creative team: Karin Wiberg and her team at Clear Sight Books, Bill Harper and the team at wmHarper Agency, and Patricia Saxton of Saxton Studio.

Thank you to my powerhouse readers, including clients, colleagues, and family: Evan Carroll, Glenn Gautier, Fana Horenbein, Scott Morgan, Barbara Petzen, Chris Quinn, Marcey Rader, Stephen G. Scotti, Jr., Michele Vargas, Ben Wechsler, and John Zikias.

Thank you to my powerhouse clients who allowed me to share their fears and successes, wins and losses, triumphs and lessons learned—you truly talk on water.

These acknowledgments would be incomplete without recognizing both Dr. Robert ("The Haak") Haakenson and Angelo Giambusso. The Haak's mentoring nurtured my passion for communications and set the trajectory for my career. And Uncle Ang has always been in my corner, guiding and encouraging me through career-defining moments. Thank you.

Stephanie Scotti has dedicated her career to preparing business leaders for high-stakes events. Her rich professional history began the moment she accepted her college degree and took a position at the largest federal speakers' bureau in the nation. At the age of twenty-four, she began working with key policymakers, including the President's Cabinet, preparing them to speak on energy policy.

Since those early years Stephanie has consulted with thousands of global executives and high-level leaders in diverse sectors ranging from high-tech, pharmaceutical, and financial services to convenience stores, retail, and lifestyle. Her insightful approach enables her clients to consistently outperform the competition, win new business, gain recognition, and influence decision makers.

Stephanie has taught at Duke University, has coached TEDxRaleigh speakers, and was named a winner of the Enterprising Women of the Year Award. She is a regular contributor to *SmartBrief Leadership* and has published articles in *Huffington Post, Business Insider,* Entrepreneur .com, and Ragan.com. She holds a bachelor's degree from James Madison University and a master's degree from Florida State University. Stephanie can be found online at professionallyspeaking.net.